Study Skills

Maximise Your Time to Pass Exams

Studymates

Studymates
Helping You to Achieve

Study Skills

Maximise Your Time to Pass Exams

John Kennedy MBA

www.studymates.co.uk

© 2005 by John Kennedy

ISBN 10 1-84 285-064-4
ISBN 13 978 1-84 285-064-0

First published in 2003 by Studymates Limited.
PO Box 2, Bishops Lydeard, Somerset TA4 3YE, United Kingdom.

Website: http://www.studymates.co.uk

Typeset by PDQ Typesetting, Newcastle-under-Lyme
Printed and bound in Great Britain by The Baskerville Press Ltd

Contents

List of illustrations

Figures

Tables

Introduction

This book is based on the premise that success in education in general, and formal programmes of study in particular, entails three crucial elements:

- knowing what information is relevant

- knowing where to find it

- knowing how to use it effectively.

However, associated with these key elements are the important personal and academic skills illustrated in the figure below.

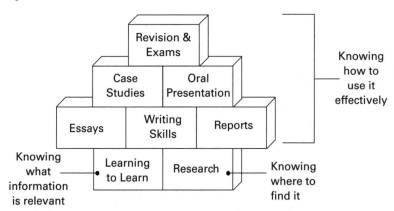

The building blocks of learning

Many students fail to realise their true potential, not because they lack ability, but because they do not possess enough expertise in areas such as planning and organising, using a library, reading skills, writing skills and examination technique. The expansion in further and higher education, and the fact that many college and university courses are now delivered in the shorter time span of the semester, has placed tremendous pressure on students. This pressure is compounded by the increasing need for students to work as well as study. All of this means that there is less time available for you to develop the key skills necessary to realise your full potential.

This book is designed to help address this situation and to enhance your personal as well as academic skills. Whether you are an 'A' level, vocational, mature or undergraduate student, this book will prove an essential aid for successful study.

John Kennedy

John_Kennedy@studymates.co.uk

1 Learning how to learn

One-minute overview

You can succeed in academic study without any detailed knowledge of the learning process. Indeed, some of your early learning experiences may have consisted of 'rote learning' (the simple repetition of key words, phrases and facts). However, as the subjects you study become more sophisticated and advanced, it becomes harder to make the most of learning opportunities without some understanding of the learning process, the factors that affect it, and how you approach and respond to learning experiences.

This chapter will help you:

■ develop a better understanding of the learning process and an increased awareness of the skills necessary for effective study and learning

■ appreciate the different ways in which people learn and identify the best method of learning for you (*your learning style*)

■ develop an awareness of the importance of planning, organising and time management

■ appreciate the value of working in groups and the valuable learning experience this provides

■ identify your main motivating factors and any potential threats to them.

1.1 The learning process

What is learning? When you understand something you did not understand before, when you know more than you knew before, or when you have developed a new skill or an appreciation for something where none existed before – then you have learned something (see Figure 1.1).

Figure 1.1
The learning
process
▶

Observing	Experimenting
Listening	Visualising
Remembering	Self-testing
Reading	Receiving feedback
Taking notes	Rhyming
Questioning	'Doing'
Linking	Making mistakes

Figure 1.1 The learning process

Learning how to learn involves:

- possessing the desire to learn and mastering the crucial skills

- understanding the learning process

- gaining an understanding of yourself as a learner, for example, your learning style (see Figure 1.3)

- overcoming blockages to learning

- effective planning and organising

- working as a member of a group

- maintaining motivation.

People who have learned how to learn have:

- developed the required knowledge, skills and attitude

- determined their main learning style and maximised their study strengths

- planned, organised and set learning objectives

- taken control of their own learning and functioned effectively in a variety of learning settings

- enjoyed learning and gained more from their time investment in the learning process.

So learning how to learn involves possessing or acquiring the knowledge, skills and ability to learn effectively in a variety of situations. Learning a subject, for example, involves three main processes:

- acquisition of information (e.g., from lectures and research)

- transformation – 'shaping' knowledge to make it relevant to new tasks and situations (e.g., writing essays and making presentations)

- evaluation – checking that the former two processes have been carried out successfully and evaluating what you have learned.

Other key elements in the learning process are understanding, memorising and 'doing'.

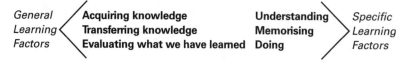

| General Learning Factors | **Acquiring knowledge** **Transferring knowledge** **Evaluating what we have learned** | **Understanding** **Memorising** **Doing** | Specific Learning Factors |

Key skills

As Figure 1.2 shows, a number of skills are crucial to learning.

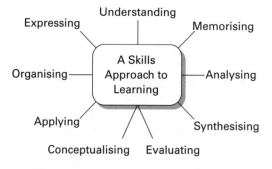

Figure 1.2 Key skills

- **Understanding:** an active mental process that enables you to put together information in a way that helps you make sense of ideas, concepts, theories and so on.

- **Memorising:** retaining and recalling information.

- **Analysing:** arriving at an understanding by examining the individual parts of a topic, theory, task or problem ('breaking things down').

- **Synthesising:** arriving at an understanding through examining the larger structure ('putting it together').

- **Evaluating:** making a value judgement.

- **Conceptualising:** linking or classifying particular items of information or knowledge to create an overall idea or meaningful whole (generalising from particular examples).

- **Applying:** putting theory into practice ('doing it').

- **Organising:** putting things into a logical, efficient and effective order.

- **Expressing:** presenting information clearly, concisely and logically, both verbally and in writing.

1.2 Learning style

'Learning style' describes the way in which a person approaches learning and his or her behaviour and activities during the learning process. Through experience, you recognise which particular learning strategies are successful for you.

There are different categories of learning style: 'enthusiastic', 'imaginative', 'practical' and 'logical'. For example, people who are enthusiastic tend to be impulsive and accept ideas readily, whereas those who are imaginative take time to consider and evaluate new ideas and experiences.

Key questions
Ask yourself whether you:

- plan your study periods carefully or start 'straight in'

- prioritise study tasks or take them as they come

- set specific learning goals and objectives or take work as it comes

- research thoroughly or prefer to enlarge upon your own ideas

- accept ideas or theories that appeal to you or look for supporting evidence

- need masses of information before you get down to work

- keep going until you 'drop' or take planned breaks.

Learning Style	Positive	Negative
Enthusiastic	Works quickly Works intuitively Tries new ideas Reads quickly	Little advance planning Attempts too many tasks Important details missed Not selective with notes
Imaginative	Innovative thinker Takes time Links study areas Interesting formats	Poor time management Accepts ideas too readily Slow to get started Easily distracted
Practical	Sets goals Can apply theory Researches well Meets deadlines	Can lack imagination Can fail to see links Preoccupied with details Prefers own ideas
Logical	Good critical powers Organises well Precise & thorough Prioritises work	Led mainly by logic Tends to be uncreative Can get lost in theory Needs a lot of information

Most education and training courses reflect 'accepted' learning styles, not the learning styles of individuals. Asking yourself these key questions and considering the factors outlined in Figure 1.3 will help you develop an awareness of the possible pitfalls associated with different approaches to study, and will enable you to make the most of your particular learning style. However, it is important to note that your style may change as your learning circumstances change. Your preferred learning style may also include aspects of the other styles illustrated.

Figure 1.3 Learning style

1.3 Planning and organising

Planning and organising your time efficiently enables you to break up long periods of academic study into realistic and achievable objectives. Planned, regular and sustained periods of study (with appropriate breaks) are usually more effective than short, irregular cramming sessions. If you make a study plan and keep to it, this will help you to make the most of formal and private study. You will find time for research and will submit work on time, having identified potential problems. Because you are keeping to your study plan you will find it also allows you to experience regular achievement, which is essential to maintain motivation if your course is a long one.

*Figure 1.4
Planning and
organising*
▼

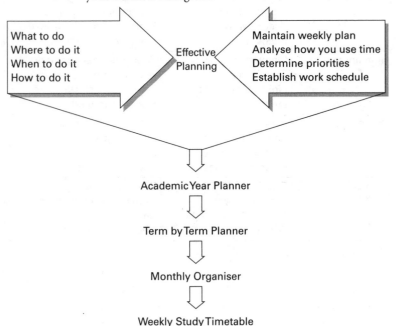

| What to do
Where to do it
When to do it
How to do it | Effective
Planning | Maintain weekly plan
Analyse how you use time
Determine priorities
Establish work schedule |

Academic Year Planner

Term by Term Planner

Monthly Organiser

Weekly Study Timetable

One of the first stages in the planning process is to familiarise yourself with your intended course or courses.

Key questions

- Is there a scheme of work for the subject?

- How many assignments are there and when are they due?

- What lectures and seminars are there?

- When are the term tests and/or end of year exams?

You must transfer the answers to these questions to your planning aids, and you must also consider what preparations you need to make. For instance, many students do not realise that not only do they have to prepare papers for seminars, they may also have to present them verbally (see Chapter 7). Another important factor is the amount of private study time required. Although this varies between individuals and subjects, you need to increase your private study significantly when exams are near. Organising for study also involves:

- planning for research, written work, revision and general study activities

- prioritising tasks and preparing action lists

- keeping work files and notes up-to-date

- balancing the time requirements of essays, projects and other course elements.

What to do and when to do it are important features of planning and organisation. But where to do it (your *learning environment*) can have a considerable influence on the quality of work produced.

The two principal aspects of the learning environment are the 'public' environment you share with other students, such as the lecture room or library, and the more private environment of your home or student accommodation. Although you have little control over the former, make sure that you:

- arrive at lectures early to ensure a good seat

- can hear the lecturer clearly

- can see any visual material without difficulty

- receive copies of all handouts and/or lecture notes

- make a note of any words or terms you do not understand and clarify these at the earliest opportunity (use the additional advice given in the section on note-taking).

Private study

Whether you study in your bedroom or in another room, make sure that you always study in this area. It is your study space – you will have all your study aids and materials close at hand and it will provide you with the right atmosphere.

Checklist: private study

Make sure you have:

- good natural and artificial light

- sufficient heating and ventilation

- a comfortable chair and enough desk space to work on (both at the right height for you)

- an academic planner and personal study timetable

- reference materials conveniently stored

- minimal noise and distraction (if music helps you study, choose the appropriate volume).

Time management

An important element of effective planning and organisation is time management. Many students underestimate the amount of time required for successful study. Even those who get it right often have to juggle the demands of an academic course with outside commitments, such as work or the family (or both). One way of assessing the demands on your time is to conduct a *time audit* (an analysis of your current use of time in general).

Key questions

- How effectively are you managing your time at college, home or work – are you controlling time or is time controlling you?

- How much of your time is controlled by others, consumed by events, or is 'free'?

- Is there any particular activity that occupies a lot of your time?

You may have little control over the demands of your home. But in the areas of work, study and other activities there are many instances where time management could be made more effective. Figure 1.5 provides a framework in which to conduct a general time audit.

Activity	% of Total Time Spent
Work	....
Home	....
Other	....
Free time	....

Figure 1.5 General time audit ◄

You also need to examine how you spend your time within each area. Figure 1.6 provides a framework for a college time audit.

Activity	% of Time Spent
Lectures	....
Tutorials	....
Research	....
Assignments	....
Other	....

Figure 1.6 College time audit ◄

The results of Figure 1.5 can be used as a rough guide to assess the relationship between your time investment in college and your other time-consuming activities. Is there a link between this time allocation and your current academic performance? Similarly, examining the results of Figure 1.6 may enable you to identify learning activities where new priorities and improvements need to be made. For example:

- Are you using lectures effectively?

- Does the time spent in research pay dividends?

- Are your assignments on time and getting good grades?

Figure 1.7 Strategies to improve time management ▼

As Figure 1.7 indicates, simple strategies can be devised to improve time management and set realistic priorities.

Task priority (state task)	Time priority (specify date)
Very important	Must be done immediately...
Important	Must be done by...
Less important	When time allows

Another useful framework for assessing such things as plans, tasks and time allocation is the 'SWOT' approach (Figure 1.8).

Time investment: key areas	Strengths	Weaknesses	Opportunities	Threats
Essays	I use time well	Takes me ages to get started	Use reading week to practise	Assessed essay due soon

▲ *Figure 1.8 The SWOT approach*

Key questions

- What are your current strengths and weaknesses?

- How could you use your time management strengths to improve your learning opportunities and academic performance?

- If any weaknesses have been identified, how do you intend overcoming them? What is your action plan?

To maximise your learning opportunities, you must plan your study using a framework such as a study timetable. Timetables should be used flexibly, allowing for lost study time to be made up or for study hours to increase when exams are due. Figure 1.9 shows a sample study timetable on A4 paper, with blank cells for inserting the particular study and time periods. It is important to include leisure and other activities. This can also easily be produced using a spreadsheet.

Figure 1.9
Example of a
study timetable
▼

	Mon	Tues	Wed	Thur	Fri	Sat	Sun
9.00							
10.00							
11.00							
12.00							
1.00							

Time management consists of common sense and a methodical approach to how you use time. It means identifying your particular *time bandits* and developing strategies to overcome them. Time bandits include too much socialising, poor research skills, a weak study style, lack of motivation, setting unrealistic goals and so on.

Checklist: time management
You need to:

- develop a personal sense of time

- make effective use of committed time

- establish a general work system

- use study aids such as term planners and study timetables

- plan your study day – prioritise

- limit socialising

- set objectives (but make them realistic)

- review your progress regularly.

Focus points: planning and organising

- Develop a study programme but build in flexibility (e.g., leisure pursuits).

- Study to suit your personal circumstances (e.g., allow for part-time work and learning style).

- Develop a comprehensive work system, for example, a research information base (your notes) on a subject-by-subject basis.

- Highlight assignment deadlines and work systematically towards them.

- Don't neglect subjects you are good at to concentrate on weak areas. Work methodically across all subjects.

- Adopt a logical approach and carry out one study task at a time (unless certain information is not available, for example, and you need to work at another element of a particular study task).

- Compile work lists and cross off each study task as it is completed. Not only is this a methodical approach, but it also gives you a sense of achievement.

1.4 Working in groups

The phrase 'each of us is not as smart as all of us' highlights the value of working in groups. Working in groups provides valuable learning experiences, and like other aspects of education and training, it has become increasingly important in recent years. A vital skill much valued by employers, the ability to work effectively in groups is now a part of many courses. It is important to distinguish between the different kinds of groups that students may be involved in:

- **Study groups.** These are formed by students themselves, mainly to research, compare notes or revise. Although a common knowledge or information base may result, assignments and so on are mostly tackled on an individual basis.

- **Tutor-appointed groups.** Membership of these groups is determined by the tutor. Specific assignments or tasks are allocated to them, and how the members function as a group often forms part of the assessment criteria.

- **Specific task groups.** Students are allowed to form groups in response to specific assignments or tasks. They can disband when the tasks are completed, but if the students find they work well together they can continue to tackle other group assignments.

Groups have advantages over individual learning methods:

- each person's knowledge, skills and expertise can be combined

- problem-solving and decision-making capabilities can be improved

- new ideas and working methods are more readily accepted

- individual confidence and self-respect can be increased

- a common sense of purpose can improve morale and motivation.

Focus points: working in groups

Although assignments in education and training are largely designed to test individual competence, some will seek to assess the ability to work effectively as a member of a group. This involves the capacity to:

- clarify group aims and objectives

- listen and be sensitive to others

- freely exchange information

- evaluate ideas or options

- use resources effectively

- objectively assess your behaviour/contribution

- generate a list of ideas/options

- criticise ideas or options constructively

- include everyone, especially weak members

- accept responsibility for tasks and deadlines

- jointly solve problems and reach decisions

- undertake a variety of roles, such as leading, following, enabling and supporting.

1.5 Group interaction

No matter how reasonable group members may be as individuals, conflict or potential conflict is often unavoidable during the life of most groups. There are several ways of dealing with this:

1 **Perceive it.** Be perceptive and try to identify as early as possible any negative comments or non-verbal behaviour which may indicate that conflict is not far away. It is also useful if you have a number of strategies you can implement, such as 3 and 4 below.

2 **Ignore it.** People sometimes try to ignore conflict in the hope that it might go away. This rarely works, and if it does, only for a short period of time.

3 **Defuse it.** A number of approaches can be used:

- declare the points to be minor or unimportant, and therefore not worth arguing about

- give way to the problem member on certain points (so he or she feels they are 'winning')

- drop the issue causing problems and return to it later (thus letting tempers cool).

4 **Confront it.** Confronting conflict can bring about three main situations:

- win-lose – one side wins and the other, of course, loses

- lose-lose – you can't win but neither can they (stalemate)

- win-win – the most positive way of resolving conflict; compromise ensures that those involved in the conflict achieve some of their individual objectives.

Conflict can also be minimised by:

- **Welcoming.** Seek other viewpoints and respond positively, even if you disagree with them.

- **Giving.** Share any information or resources you may have.

- **Persuading.** Convince others by being persuasive rather than dominant or aggressive.

- **Circumventing.** Ignore destructive comments or behaviour and seek contributions from constructive group members.

- **'Building'.** Build on the positive comments from constructive group members.

- **Limiting.** Place a time limit on individual comments.

Checklist: working in groups
Make your group-work more effective by ensuring that:

- objectives are understood and accepted by everyone

- views are sought from each member

- discussion includes everyone, especially shy members

- criticism is encouraged and is constructive when made

- decisions are arrived at through agreement

- someone is co-ordinating

- a plan of action has been drawn up

- deadlines have been set

- tasks have been allocated (fairly) to each member

- everyone has a copy of crucial documents and information

- each member is contributing

- discussions are not being monopolised by anyone

- serious conflict is avoided.

1.6 Motivation

People are motivated to study:

- for the satisfaction and sense of achievement that study can bring

- because they have developed an interest in a particular subject

- to give them a 'second chance' if they have been unable to make the most of their previous formal learning experiences

- to enhance their life chances, particularly where their career is concerned.

Figure 1.10 Motivation ▶

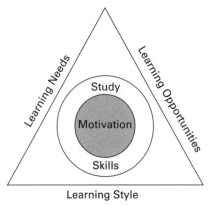

Focus points: threats to motivation

Threats to motivation include:

- prior learning experiences (negative)

- increased independence regarding study (can I cope on my own?)

- higher expectations in terms of the work produced (am I up to it?)

- an increase in the volume of work (I can't meet all the deadlines)

- not getting the grades expected

- moving away from home (though some students yearn for independence)

- self-generated fears (e.g., I cannot afford to fail).

Checklist: maintaining motivation

One of the best ways of maintaining motivation is to identify your main motivators, be aware of the main threats to them and develop strategies such as:

- good planning and organisation, especially where research and assignment deadlines are concerned

- developing sound study skills

- not over-reacting when you do not get the grade expected

- responding to/seeking tutors comments on the work produced

- aiming to do well, but not setting yourself unrealistic expectations (this increases stress as well as affecting motivation)

- adopting a positive attitude (I am a conscientious student, I work hard, I am going to succeed).

Summary

- Learning to learn involves possessing, or acquiring, the knowledge, skills and ability to learn effectively in a variety of situations.

- Learning itself involves a number of processes such as acquiring knowledge (from lectures, for example), transferring it to new tasks and situations (e.g., writing essays) and evaluating what you have learned.

● A number of skills crucial to learning can be identified, such as: understanding, memorising, analysing, synthesising, evaluating, conceptualising, 'applying', organising and expressing.

● Approaches to learning (your learning style) are closely linked to understanding.

● Preparing and working to plan helps you to:

– make the most of formal and private study

– research and submit work on time

– identify potential study problems

– experience a daily sense of achievement.

● Working in groups provides valuable learning experiences.

● Groups have advantages over individual learning methods: the knowledge, skills and expertise of each member can be combined; and problem-solving and decision-making capabilities can be improved.

● One of the best ways of maintaining motivation is to identify what your main motivators are, be aware of the main threats to them and develop strategies to meet these threats.

Tutorial

1 Think of a successful learning experience you have had in the past, and ask yourself the following questions:

● What were the main factors about the task that interested you?

● Did you feel challenged or 'stretched'?

- Was it possible to learn in your own way?

- What role (if any) did others play in helping you to learn, and what was your reaction to them?

- What problems did you encounter, and how did you overcome them?

- How did you feel when you finished the task?

Carrying out the above exercise enables you to reflect on:

- the type of learning task and its relevance to you (what value you placed upon this learning experience, and hence what you might value about learning in general)

- how such learning experiences may have affected your attitude towards learning in general

- your attitude towards the involvement of others in your learning experiences (your ability to work successfully with others in the learning context)

- your approach to problem-solving and analysis

- your study style

- how important achievement is to you as a motivator

- your ability to apply prior learning experiences to future learning tasks.

2 Were you ever a member of a group that was ineffective? Using the material in the 'Working in groups' section, try to find out why. What strategies would you now adopt to overcome such difficulties?

3 Using the self-assessment checklist on the next page, try to assess your actual or potential behaviour in groups. What changes (if any) do you need to make in order to be more effective?

Self-assessment of group behaviour

I try to:	Rarely	Sometimes	Often
Provide relevant information	...	...	...
Clarify objectives	...	...	...
Make relevant and positive suggestions	...	...	...
Provide leadership where appropriate	...	...	...
Keep the group 'on course'	...	...	...
Refrain from 'winning' behaviour	...	...	...
Support other group members	...	...	...
Resolve conflict constructively	...	...	...
Acknowledge the expertise of other group members	...	...	...

Other personal behaviour noted

....

....

....

....

....

Personal action plan: improving group skills

I must try to:

1 ....

2 ....

3 ....

4 ....

5 ....

6 ....

2 **Routine research**

One-minute overview

Carrying out research is necessary for most academic work. Skills such as the ability to write well are essential but the quality of essays, assignments and other assessed activities is always improved if the subject is thoroughly researched. Research can be divided into two categories: routine research; and the more extensive research required for special projects such as an undergraduate dissertation.

Routine research requires you to be systematic, make notes, use facilities such as the library and analyse written texts.

This chapter will help you to:
- develop an efficient recording system
- use library resources effectively
- get the most from textbooks and other written material
- develop your reading skills
- choose a note-taking method that works for you
- anticipate and overcome potential problems
- select a research topic
- prepare a research outline
- understand the key issues involved in the various research methods.

2.1 Establishing a system

For any type of research an organised and efficient system for recording information is essential. Index cards and storage boxes are available from most high-street stationers. Alternatively, A4 sheets can be used. These have the advantage that diagrams and other visual information can be added, and they can be kept in an appropriately indexed ring binder. Whichever method you use, it is important that the following information is recorded:

- the author's full name (or initials and surname)

- date of publication

- title (underlined)

- place of publication

- publisher

- the general theme

- main points of interest

- any additional subject references

- any additional points or questions the information raises

- any links to existing notes, for example, 'see index card 6'.

Authors	Smith, J. & Webster, R.	Year of publication	2003
Title of book	Modern Economics	Dewey decimal no.	330.111
Place of publication	London	Name of publisher	Publications Ltd
International Standard Book Number	ISBN 0 666 12345 6		
General theme (Chapter 2)...			
Main points...			
Additional comments..			

Figure 2.1
Sample index
card

For books, it is useful to note the Dewey decimal number and the International Standard Book Number (ISBN). The Dewey decimal system is the main classification system used in the UK. It is usually found on the spine of the book (for example, 658.111 KEN), and once you have obtained the Dewey decimal number from the library index it quickly helps you to locate a particular book in the correct part of the library. Every publication has its own ISBN number, therefore if you are requesting a book either in a bookshop or from a library it is helpful to know it.

You should record more detailed information for journals because they appear more frequently than books. As well as the title and the year of publication, you should note the volume, issue and page numbers. For example, *Economic Journal*, vol. 5 (2) indicates that this is the fifth year the journal has been published and this is the second issue within that year. If any detailed notes (such as quotes) are made from books or journals, it is good practice to state the page number(s).

Noting details about sources of information is not just good practice and necessary for your research, it also provides supporting evidence for the final piece of work you produce.

Checklist: system
You should:

● select one recording method and stick to it

● have relevant queries and search categories

● take a 'first thoughts' approach to focus your research (these can be developed later)

● note any new points or questions your research raises

● devise a separate coding system for each subject

● check for any links with existing notes

● note anything you believe to be relevant

● date each separate piece of research

- take the identifying details of the item you are researching (e.g., the Dewey decimal number and ISBN where books are concerned).

2.2 Using the library

Some students look only on the library shelves. This is not a good idea, because they will be unaware of other relevant books that may be available. For instance, important books in their research subject area may be out on loan, or new books may be being processed by library staff.

Students also sometimes underestimate the value of libraries. The introduction of modern technology such as computer systems, microfilm and microfiche means that libraries have become even more valuable as an information source for research (see Figure 2.2).

Figure 2.2 Services provided by libraries ▶

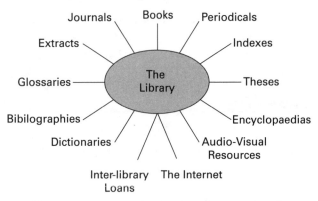

Whether they use a card index or a computer-based system, most libraries divide their catalogues into three main sections: title, author and subject.

Another important part of the library is the reference section. This contains valuable sources such as bibliographies, indexes and abstracts. Some of the useful reference works your library might contain are:

- British National Bibliography (lists all the new books published in the UK)

- British Humanities Index

- Social Sciences Index

- Nursing Bibliography

- Personnel and Training Abstracts (ANBAR)

- Catalogue of British Official Publications

- Social Trends (useful statistics published by the Central Statistical Office)

- Clover Newspaper Index.

When researching a subject, remember to widen your search terms. For example, if you are researching a project on *business communication* you will automatically limit the number of potential sources if you concentrate solely on these two words. However, if you widen the search to include other terms, such as those listed below, you will generate a lot more useful information:

- management skills

- people skills

- business organisations

- training

- customer care

- organisational behaviour

- employee relations

- public relations

- communication skills.

Checklist: library

You are advised to:

- familiarise yourself with the facilities your college or university library offers (it may provide a library guide)

- check what facilities you may have to pay for (e.g., inter-library loans)

- familiarise yourself with the sections concerning your subjects (but not exclusively so)

- use the expertise of the librarians. They are trained professionals and very approachable, and they may have specific expertise in your chosen subject areas

- use the Dewey or any other classification system provided

- find out how the lending system works (how many books can you have at once and for how long?)

- find out if there is a short loan system and how it works (is there a fine for overdue books?)

- use a logical and efficient system to record the books you have referred to.

2.3 Getting the most from textbooks

Before reading any textbook, be clear about why you need to read it (*reading strategy*). The key questions below should help you clarify your reading strategy.

Key questions

- Do I need more detailed information? (Answers to questions such as what, where, when, why, how, who.)

- Do I need a wider understanding of the issue? (Further and more comprehensive reading required.)

- Are contrasting viewpoints necessary? (More balanced approach.)

- Do I need key terms explained? (Detailed reading.)

- Am I looking for suitable quotations to use as evidence? (Specific reading.)

The three-step model below may help you save valuable reading time by outlining a methodical approach.

Step 1: General appraisal (does the book appear to be useful?)

check:

- the preface/foreword etc.

- the date of publication (is it up-to-date?)

- the footnotes (if any) and bibliography.

Step 2: Focusing (to find information quickly or gain an overview)

check:

- the table of contents (first and last paragraphs of chapters)

- chapter summaries (first and last sentences of paragraphs)

- the index (for key words and phrases).

Step 3: Fact finding (detailed reading)

check:

- whole sentences

- whole paragraphs and sections

- specific details.

Other important aspects of the 'why' reading strategy are reading for criticism and reading for understanding. Both are crucial for developing a deeper understanding of your chosen subject(s) and for conveying this understanding to others.

Reading for criticism (is it objective?)

check:

- what points or conclusions are not supported by facts

- whether facts are used selectively

- could other claims or conclusions be equally valid?

Reading for understanding

check:

- that you've set yourself a reading deadline (stop when you've reached it)

- that you're reading with a purpose (prepare a list of questions)

- that you have reviewed any notes you have on the subject (this will prevent duplication and time-wasting).

Reading speed

This is something else that can create concern for students. Faster readers often read in 'word clusters' and reduce the number of eye contacts ('fixtures'), as shown in Figure 2.3.

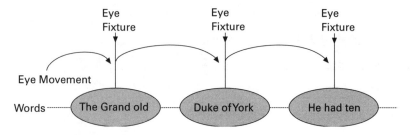

Figure 2.3
Reading
speed

Focus points: reading quickly

Try to:

- help your eyes to see more (read in word clusters)

- concentrate on the key points/main ideas (look for key words and phrases)

- reduce going back over passages as much as possible (unless you are reading for specific details)

- avoid 'vocalising' i.e. speaking the words to yourself as you are reading

- build up your speed over a period of time (practise on material such as newspapers)

- keep a regular log of your reading speed (words per minute).

But remember that:

- increased reading speed is pointless if your understanding suffers

- your reading speed will be affected by your reading strategy (such as whether you are examining key terms or looking for quotes). It could be reduced to 40–50 words per minute.

Indicator words

The way certain words or phrases are used can help you understand the flow of the text and grasp the main ideas. *Slow-down* words such as 'however', 'nevertheless', 'although' and 'rather' indicate that a change of ideas is about to occur. *Keep-going* words such as 'furthermore', 'indeed' and 'moreover' signal that there is more of the same. Lastly, *here-it-comes* words such as 'therefore', 'consequently', 'accordingly' and 'thus' show that a summary or conclusion is imminent. These indicator words are also extremely useful in written work.

SQ3R

One method of reading is called the SQ3R method (survey, question, read, recall, review). You may find the SQ3R checklist that follows helpful.

Checklist: SQ3R reading

Survey   – check the date of the publication

           – read the preface/introduction and contents page

           – read chapter headings

	– look at the index and bibliography
Question	– what points are you specifically interested in?
	– create questions (questions of association are vital)
	– what? where? when? why? how? who?
Read	– what are the main ideas/key points?
	– read each chapter at least twice (look for key words and phrases)
	– is there evidence for the author's ideas?
	– what consequences flow from the author's ideas/theories?
Recall	– try to recall all the main ideas and key points
	– make notes
	– what can you remember without notes?
Review	– check everything!

2.4 Taking notes

Although taking notes from lectures is largely a reactive process (you simply respond to the lecturer speaking), and therefore does not really constitute research, it is linked to research in several ways:

● you are benefiting from the research the lecturer has conducted

● important references and further reading may be given during lectures

● lecture notes form part of your research base

● taking notes in lectures develops the crucial note-taking skills necessary for effective research.

Students often become anxious when trying to take notes from lectures for the first time. This can be made worse if:

- the lecturer talks too fast

- the lecturer talks when you are trying to take notes

- you do not know what comments to take down

- panic sets in and the whole process becomes a blur.

These problems can be overcome through experience, but the best way is to develop your own strategies and note-taking method. In developing your strategies, the following may be useful:

1 **Practise active listening.** Listen for implied meaning (certain facts are not 'spelt out') in respect of comments made, or make mental links between previous notes or study periods. This can be quite tiring since it calls for maximum concentration.

2 **Listen for key words or phrases.** Use your listening skills to identify linking words or phrases (even jokes) from vital learning points. For example, during a marketing lecture a business student might hear 'The four most important elements of the marketing mix are ...'. These are not the significant words, of course, but the ones that follow – 'product, price, place and promotion' – are.

3 **Look for non-verbal cues.** As you are taking crucial notes, the lecturer may point to the board, overhead projector or other teaching aid to emphasise or make a key point. Different hand signals or other aspects of non-verbal behaviour may also be used to reinforce key points.

4 **Be alert for 'indicator words'.** These include 'however', 'furthermore', 'accordingly', 'finally'.

5 **Be participative.** Ask questions which consolidate or clarify your notes. This may not be possible in large lecture halls, but take the opportunity in any follow-up tutorials or seminars.

6 **Note what you don't understand as well as what you do.** Follow up these points as soon as possible with the lecturer concerned.

7 **Develop your own 'shorthand' system.** Figure 2.4 illustrates how you may shorten the phrase 'government and politics' as you become more familiar with the topic. However, it is not enough to merely shorten the original words because, after the lecture, you may be left with a lot of abbreviations but little understanding of the original meaning. The crucial part of the exercise is to make a list (as soon as possible after the lecture) of what the abbreviations mean. This may seem a lot of extra work but it will enhance your understanding of the original notes: first, by processing the material several times; and second, by 'translating' the ideas and concepts of others into your own words.

Figure 2.4 Using shorthand for familiar phrases ▶

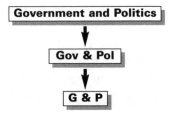

As Figure 2.5 indicates, mind maps or pattern notes have significant advantages over traditional notes (those written in sentences):

● they are more easily remembered than sentences

● they reflect the relationships between ideas

● new ideas can be integrated into existing notes

● the key-word and phrase approach means that they are quicker to write and read.

Under the pressure of academic work students may take notes and then forget about them until assignments or examinations are due. Another mistake is to view note-taking as a temporary (for example, for specific assignments) and passive process. To make note-taking pay dividends:

- view it as an active process and make your notes work for you

- establish a notes information base

- see it as system of 'inputs' and 'outputs'

- see it as a vital academic tool and life-long skill.

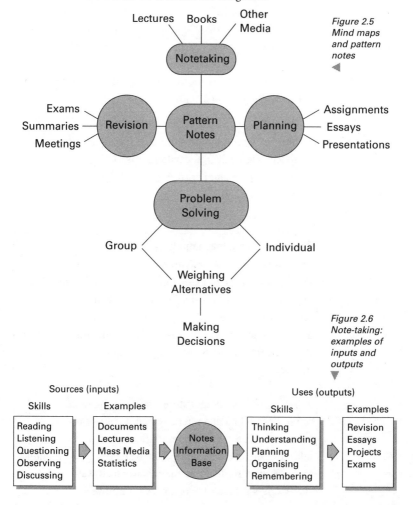

Figure 2.5
Mind maps and pattern notes

Figure 2.6
Note-taking: examples of inputs and outputs

Checklist: note-taking

It helps to:

● use a variety of sources

● look or listen for key words

● select a note-taking method which suits you (see pages 32 and 33)

● establish a notes information base

● use a variety of methods to highlight key points, such as colours, underlining, capital letters, spacing

● constantly update and revise your notes

● make your notes work for you; view them in terms of inputs and outputs.

The following fictitious extract gives an idea of how a business student might take notes using the traditional approach (Figure 2.7), the pattern approach (Figure 2.8) and the compare and contrast approach (points for and against, Figure 2.9).

Chapter 4: The importance of 'people skills'

Managers have little hesitation in helping staff to develop their people skills, but sometimes neglect to develop these key skills themselves. A recent case involving a large UK retail organisation confirms repeated research that the attitude of managers towards staff is of vital importance if the sometimes hidden but costly consequences are to be avoided

Although store A and store B were in the same county town, store B had an extremely high turnover of employees; in some cases, they left without notice. In addition, there was a higher than average sickness rate for this size of store. To make matters worse, it was increasingly difficult to recruit new employees.

A senior manager from head office was sent to investigate store B, but decided first to call unannounced at store A. Here, he found the store manager to be highly regarded by all employees. Upon entering the manager's room he found the door wedged open and a checkout operator leaving a number of suggestions as to how queues could be reduced at peak times. When questioned, the checkout operator told the senior manager that her visit was not unusual, everyone was encouraged to make suggestions.

Further discussions with a range of employees including supervisors and section managers confirmed that the store manager communicated regularly with all staff; was on the shop floor regularly and helped at busy times; developed them by delegating authority in an appropriate way; respected them as individuals as well as employees; and persuaded them to do work they didn't have to, rather than order them to do it.

It was clear to the senior manager that the manager of store A was highly respected by his employees and had encouraged them to view change as an opportunity. The senior manager was in no doubt that the excellent people skills of manager A was the reason why his store performed so well and the employees were so highly motivated.

Unfortunately, the senior manager's visit to store B was not so positive. Almost as he entered store B he found staff complaining about a number of issues, including: being ordered by the manager to do things they didn't have to do; dealing with customer complaints because the manager would not leave his office; not having enough information to do their jobs; and the manager refusing to listen to suggestions which could improve things. Tension among the employees and little respect for manager B were evident.

Although supervisors and section managers tried to be loyal, it was apparent to the senior manager that the employees' comments he overheard were an accurate reflection of the situation. The senior manager went to speak to the manager of store B. He confirmed to the senior manager that he communicated mainly through his section managers and discouraged visits and suggestions from 'ordinary employees'. He also stated that he felt managers should keep their authority and not delegate it. Further comments from manager B revealed that he thought employees needed to know who was boss ('after all, the position of manager commands respect').

Whereas store manager A welcomed change, store manager B viewed it as 'creating problems'. It was clear to the senior manager that because morale was so low, everyday problems became a series of crises. The obvious stress the manager was under simply worsened the situation.

Fortunately, store B manager had some holiday due, which would allow him to leave his own store without being undermined. However, the senior manager was in no doubt that the store B manager would need some 'awareness-raising' about his overall approach to people, guidance from experienced 'people skills' managers and a period of retraining.

Figure 2.7
Traditional
notes
▶

Title:	Managing Effectively – Developing People Skills
Authors:	Scott, P. & Green, B.
Dewey no.	658.000 Sco
Theme of Chapter 4:	Some managers fail to realise the negative effects of poor people skills
Main points:	

1 Managers have little hesitation in helping staff to develop their 'people skills', but sometimes neglect to develop these key skills themselves.

2 Lack of people skills can result in serious problems such as lack of respect for management, tension amongst employees and low morale.

3 In addition to obvious problems such as tension etc., there are also hidden and costly consequences:

- Employees don't have enough information to do their job

- Potential improvements don't happen

- Problems often become a crisis

- High sickness rates and people leaving.

Figure 2.8
Pattern notes

Problem
Manager neglects key people skills

Obvious signs
- Lack of respect
- Tension
- Low morale
- Problem = crisis

Hidden costs
- Not enough info. to do the job
- Little improvement or change
- High sickness rates and staff leaving

Made worse by increased stress of manager

Solution
* Awareness-raising
* Guidance
* Training

4 A number of possible solutions include awareness-raising about handling people, guidance from experienced colleagues, and training in 'people skills'

Figure 2.9
Compare and contrast notes

Manager A	Manager B
Communicates regularly with everyone	Limited communication, mostly other managers
Helps when staff under pressure	Rarely seen out of his office
Seen as approachable by all employees	Discourages visits from 'ordinary employees'
Delegates authority and encourages all workers to accept responsibility	Won't delegate and believes that employees should know who's boss
Motivates his employees	Demotivates staff and causes tension

Sees respect as a two-way process	Believes managers should command respect
Prefers to persuade employees to do some tasks voluntarily	Orders employees to do work they don't have to do
Views change as an opportunity	Sees change as a threat, as 'creating problems'

▲

Figure 2.9 Compare and contrast notes (contd)

Focus points: compare and contrast notes

Compare and contrast notes:

- enable facts and data to be compared and contrasted

- help reveal links across key areas

- assist with essay and assignment preparation

- improve revision and examination preparation.

You should try to use the different styles of note-taking shown above. Do not use one method exclusively.

2.5 Special projects
Common problems

While carrying out an extended piece of research has always been the practice at undergraduate level and above, similar research is increasingly being used at other levels. Many courses encourage students to study a practical problem in school/college or in the workplace, conduct related analysis, and offer recommendations or solutions. For students who have little or no experience of how to conduct research, this can be daunting. Whatever the level of study, students can experience a number of problems:

1 **The self-fulfilling prophecy.** In an extensive project such as an undergraduate thesis, a hypothesis may be stated and then an investigation carried out to confirm the hypothesis. A hypothesis is a sort of informed guess about the possible relationship between certain factors, data, or variables. However, there is an inherent danger – a hypothesis may become a self-fulfilling prophecy. In other words, students consciously or unconsciously 'find' the evidence to prove the original theory.

2 **The hope strategy.** Students commence without a hypothesis but with some general idea of what they are trying to achieve. This problem is the reverse of the one above: instead of the research theory determining the study, the study determines the research. Accordingly, they may generate mountains of research in the hope that some concrete idea will emerge to enable them to put the research to good use.

3 **Lack of planning.** Students increasingly have to cope with special research as well as their usual assessed work, and there is often a feeling that current assignments are more important than the special study. They forget that, in a way, the special study is a current piece of work, only the assessment is not so immediate. Consequently, without proper planning techniques (see page 5) and clear objectives, students can find themselves in great difficulty when trying to balance routine assessed work with the demands of the special project.

4 **The false start.** Although students can meet this problem at any time (for example, with exam questions), it is particularly associated with great enthusiasm about the research topic. The researcher gets 'stuck in' without giving any real thought to important details such as information sources or other important elements. Unlike the examination situation, where the candidate has the benefit of other questions to compensate, the project researcher only has one opportunity and a rapidly approaching deadline to meet.

5 **Selecting the topic.** Although special projects offer students greater academic freedom and an added opportunity to display their knowledge and ability (a contributing factor to the 'false start' syndrome), this freedom of choice can be a problem in itself. Students may find that they have to make compromises in respect of their particular interests, their knowledge base, the actual information available and the constraint of time.

6 **Producing a proposal (research outline).** Turning the 'first thoughts' list into a research outline is not easy, particularly

when detailed research has not yet been carried out. Even when some research is conducted, the chosen categories may have to change to accommodate the findings. Nevertheless, it is vital to produce a plan of action, keep such a plan flexible and inform tutors or research supervisors of any changes (and seek their opinion).

Research stages

Figure 2.10 Typical research stages ▼

A useful way of anticipating and overcoming problems is to view the whole undertaking as a process consisting of key stages (see Figure 2.10). Time management is crucial, so approximate times should be allocated to each stage (these can be confirmed later).

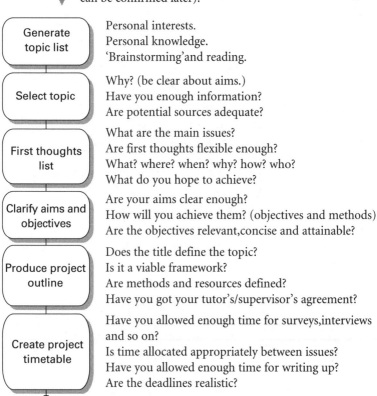

Generate topic list	Personal interests. Personal knowledge. 'Brainstorming'and reading.
Select topic	Why? (be clear about aims.) Have you enough information? Are potential sources adequate?
First thoughts list	What are the main issues? Are first thoughts flexible enough? What? where? when? why? how? who? What do you hope to achieve?
Clarify aims and objectives	Are your aims clear enough? How will you achieve them? (objectives and methods) Are the objectives relevant,concise and attainable?
Produce project outline	Does the title define the topic? Is it a viable framework? Are methods and resources defined? Have you got your tutor's/supervisor's agreement?
Create project timetable	Have you allowed enough time for surveys,interviews and so on? Is time allocated appropriately between issues? Have you allowed enough time for writing up? Are the deadlines realistic?
Commence research	

Personal checklist

One way of approaching research is to ask yourself
questions and develop a personal checklist (see Figure 2.11).

If several research tasks have to be started at the same
time, you may have additional problems. For instance, it is
not enough just to ask for information from individuals or
organisations and then wait for it to arrive; other tasks need
to be completed while you are waiting. Therefore, in
addition to a general timetable, it is useful to keep a research

*Figure 2.11
Personal
checklist*

Why am I researching this area?
What key issues will be addressed?
— Research rationale

What research do I need to conduct?
What data will I need to gather?
— Evidence

What do I hope to achieve?
How could my completed research
be used?
— Aims

How am I going to achieve my aims?
What are the key research stages?
— Objectives

How will I conduct the research?
What 'tools' will I need?
— Methodology

How will I present the findings?
— Format

diary. This enables you to anticipate problems and pursue other research tasks if difficulties arise.

Research can be such an enjoyable activity that time passes quickly, so remember to set a deadline for research to stop and writing to start. Another common problem is that students often underestimate the time it takes to prepare and proofread the final piece of work. It is important to develop a system of checking as you proceed. If you are using a computer, save data regularly, produce a hard copy as often as you can, and keep a back-up disk (update this as you work).

Selecting a topic

Various things can influence the selection of a research topic:

1 Your personal interests

2 What you know about the topic (your knowledge base)

3 The current popularity of certain themes (this should not override 1 above)

4 The research sources and information available

5 Your ability in, or preference for, certain research methods

6 The time available

One of the most effective ways to select a research topic is to brainstorm all the possible themes, on the basis of this list, then narrow down the range of potential topics until the most feasible one is selected. Figure 2.12 shows the process used to finalise the selection of a research project on recruitment and selection.

You are strongly advised to discuss the consequences of potential topics with your tutor or project supervisor. Their objectivity can be a good counterbalance to over-

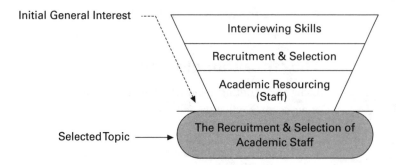

enthusiasm and their experience can help identify any elements that may cause problems. In addition to this you can:

▲
Figure 2.12
Brainstorming
themes

- make preliminary investigations to ensure that all the information you require about the topic is available

- ensure that the people who might feature in your investigations will be able to help when you need them to

- find out what impact (if any) the choice of topic will have on the research design and methods.

Checklist: topic selection

Unless your choice is clear from the outset, keep several options in mind:

- How good is your existing knowledge about the proposed topic? (Briefly write down everything you know about it.)

- Define what particular aspects you wish to explore (and why).

- Do you want to give a broad overview or concentrate on a few key issues?

- What approach might the topic indicate? (For or against? Compare and contrast? And so on)

- How many sections will there be? (Do these reflect the key issues?)

- Does the title clearly, concisely and accurately define the topic?

The 'first thoughts' list

Using the recruitment and selection of academic staff as an example, a first thoughts list might include the following:

- What makes a good lecturer?

- How is this decided?

- What procedures are used to recruit and select academic staff?

- What information do potential candidates get?

- Do the people who sit on selection panels receive any training?

The project plan (research outline)

The theme of the recruitment and selection of academic staff illustrates the form a project plan might take.

Working title: The recruitment and selection of academic staff

Aim: To examine the various factors affecting the recruitment and selection (R&S) of academic staff and, if possible, to make appropriate recommendations to improve the process

Objectives

1 To develop a list of recommended personal and professional qualities for such staff

2 To investigate and highlight examples of good practice with respect to R&S procedures

---

3 To examine the R&S procedures of my school/college and make any necessary recommendations to improve current procedures

Resources

1 People involved in the R&S of academic staff

2 Possible publications in the field

3 The procedures and practices of a suitable number of schools/colleges

Strategies

1 Examine current practice in own school/college

2 Analyse the R&S procedures in other schools/colleges

3 Identify good practice in relation to interview procedures

4 Compare and contrast general practice with that of my own school/college

Proposed methodology

Primary research (an original piece of information or data): e.g., interviews with those responsible for R&S

Secondary research ('second-hand' information): analysis of existing publications

Conducting a literature search

A literature search is a comprehensive review of published and unpublished work from secondary sources that is relevant to the research area.

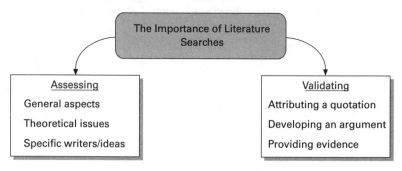

Assessing	Validating
General aspects	Attributing a quotation
Theoretical issues	Developing an argument
Specific writers/ideas	Providing evidence

Figure 2.13
The importance of literature searches

Literature searches are important because they:

● help ensure that no vital variable is ignored

● facilitate the integration of information gathered from other sources

● assist in the choice of a suitable theoretical framework.

You can use most of the ideas and suggestions in this chapter to help you plan and conduct a literature search. For instance, you will need to use cross-references and widen your search terms as suggested earlier in this chapter.

Factors such as the topic selected and research time available will impose some restrictions, but you will also have to set sensible limits. For example, there may be time constraints such as recruitment and selection in the year 2004, or categories may be quite narrow such as graduate recruitment, or international, national or regional aspects.

Although it often depends upon research circumstances and the information available, a subject-based search strategy is generally effective. Rather than spending valuable research time searching through individual books and journals, sources such as the British National Bibliography (for books) and Ulrich's International Periodicals Directory (for abstracts) allow a wider research approach to be adopted. Abstracts can save hours of research time since they provide summaries of books, articles and so on.

The internet has become an important research tool, but the search terms have to be chosen with great care.

The breadth of your search will depend on such things as the time available and the length of your final project. If you are writing a short article, for instance, you will not need to search through several theses. If you are writing a more detailed study, then most libraries will have access to lists of theses and other publications.

Checklist: literature search

Before you start:

- decide on the topic and related areas

- select the key terms – use methods such as brainstorming, pattern notes and a thesaurus

- identify any limiting factors such as the research time available, or particular constraints of the subject matter

- set research limitations (e.g., time periods, categories, and international, national or regional dimensions)

- identify potential information sources (e.g., textbooks, journals, bibliographies, abstracts, theses – look at Figure 2.2 again)

- establish a working method (review section 2.1)

- choose a referencing system and stick to it.

Research methods

There are two main approaches to data collection: quantitative and qualitative. The quantitative approach involves studying the relationship of one set of facts or data to another. It focuses on applying scientific techniques (such as statistics) to measure changes or differences so that an objective comparison can be made. The qualitative approach is used where the data is not easily measurable, placing the emphasis on how individuals perceive and make sense of the world. Thus a greater amount of human judgement and interpretation is involved.

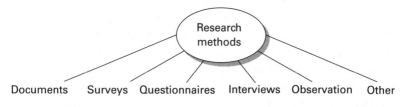

*Figure 2.14
Research
methods*

1 Documents

Most of what has been discussed in relation to textbooks applies to the examination of documents. If possible, other sources should be used to verify authenticity and any issues the documents raise.

2 Questionnaires

Designing, distributing and evaluating questionnaires involves a lot of work, so you must be certain at the outset that this is the best method for conducting your research. Look at your research outline and any preliminary reading and clarify the key issues and questions raised. If necessary, conduct a pilot survey (that is, test the survey on a few people first).

The process is as follows:

- select the survey sample (people to be questioned)
- design the questionnaire (format, content, and question type)
- code the data (if required)
- pre-test
- analyse the data.

When constructing your questionnaire, you need to consider what you need to know and how you will pose the questions. Questions can be 'open' (for example, what? where? when? why? how? who?), 'closed' (requiring a 'yes' or 'no' answer), or pre-coded to help analysis (see box). Ranking the questions and using categories are common formats used in questionnaires; categories are particularly useful for sensitive issues such as age.

A pre-coded question		
Age	18–25	[1]
Age	26–33	[2]
Age	34–41	[3]

Some problem areas include:

- asking what the respondents (those who reply to your questions) may not or cannot know

- asking complicated questions

- asking leading questions, such as 'surely you agree...'

- asking too many theoretical questions (you'll get too many theoretical answers)

- sensitive issues such as age, politics, religion and so on.

Checklist: questionnaire

A questionnaire should have:

- a brief but purposeful introduction and acknowledgement

- simple but comprehensive format

- clear instructions

- as few questions as possible

- relevant, clear and unambiguous questions

- assurance of confidentiality (if required).

3 Interviews

Interviews range from the informal to the highly structured. The format depends upon the information required and the overall nature of the research. One interview process can incorporate several interview types. Nevertheless, the more standardised the interview, the easier it is to analyse the results. The main types of interview are:

- the standardised schedule interview

Figure 2.15
Interview types
- the standardised interview with no schedule
▼
- the unstructured interview (see Figure 2.15).

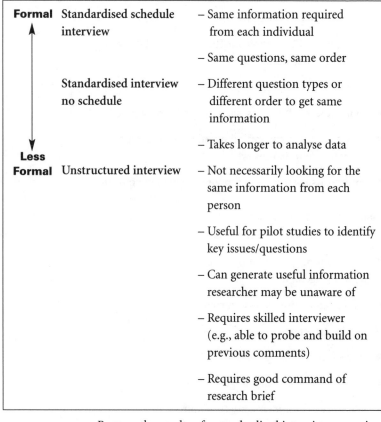

Formal ↑	Standardised schedule interview	– Same information required from each individual
		– Same questions, same order
	Standardised interview no schedule	– Different question types or different order to get same information
↓		– Takes longer to analyse data
Less Formal	Unstructured interview	– Not necessarily looking for the same information from each person
		– Useful for pilot studies to identify key issues/questions
		– Can generate useful information researcher may be unaware of
		– Requires skilled interviewer (e.g., able to probe and build on previous comments)
		– Requires good command of research brief

Because the results of a standardised interview are easier to analyse, this method is best used where a large group is involved, or where the target group share the same characteristics. Standardised interviews are also useful where the key issues are clearly understood, and the researcher is familiar with the characteristics of the interviewees.

As in the 'any other comments' part of the questionnaire, an element of freedom for the respondent to reveal feelings and issues that are important to them is useful. It can generate valuable information that may not have been thought significant. However, there is always the danger of bias and loss of control. The interviewer needs to be able to 'carry' the interview and bring it to a successful conclusion.

Checklist: interview

Before you start:

- decide on the interview type

- select a schedule or general framework (unstructured interview)

- devise a list of questions

- decide how to record data

- choose a method for data analysis

- hold a preliminary interview (to refine question type and overall approach)

- pilot test the revised format (using a small number of people).

Then you can start the interview process!

4 Observation

Research tools such as questionnaires are useful for determining people's perceptions of events. When clarification or checking is required, methods such as direct observation might be necessary. As well as the skills needed for most research, observation studies require a good understanding of what events or matters are important.

Focus points: observation

- The researcher needs to record exactly what is seen.

- The researcher needs to be able to understand what is seen.

- How often does such behaviour occur?

- How representative is it?

- The presence of the researcher may affect the behaviour being observed.

You need to decide what aspects the observation will focus on. For example, are you interested in what is achieved (content) or how it is achieved (process)? How will you record the data? How often will it be recorded?

Whatever research method is used, it must conform to two key measures:

- reliability, which is concerned with the extent to which a test or procedure produces the same result under the same conditions, and on all occasions

- validity, which relates to the extent to which the test or description is an accurate measure of the research item(s).

Summary

- It is useful to look at research in terms of routine research and the more extensive research required for a dissertation or thesis.

- Whether you are conducting routine or extensive research, an organised and efficient system for recording information is essential.

- Noting details such as the Dewey and ISBN numbers (textbooks), the author, title, place of publication and so on is not only good research practice, but is also vital for providing supporting evidence for the finished piece of work.

● Libraries are a key resource, and strategies such as cross-referencing and widening research terms are crucial for maximising potential information.

● Getting the most from textbooks involves strategies such as general appraisal, 'focusing', fact-finding, reading for understanding and reading for criticism.

● A key research skill is note-taking, which involves active listening, listening for key words and phrases, being alert for 'indicator words' and developing your own 'shorthand'.

● Conducting extensive research often entails overcoming problems such as lack of planning, selecting the topic and producing a research outline. A useful way of anticipating and overcoming problems is to view the undertaking as consisting of key stages.

● Although a variety of methods exist to help research (such as surveys, questionnaires, interviews, observation and 'critical incident' techniques) great care needs to be taken with, issues such as, research design, validity and reliability.

Tutorial

1 Select a textbook which is necessary for your course:

   a) List a number of questions or learning points which you need to clarify or develop through reading

   b) Select a chapter and state the theme briefly

   c) Make relevant traditional notes (write sentences)

   d) Convert the traditional notes into pattern notes

2 Choose a passage or text which requires you to be particularly analytical:

a) Make a series of comparative notes ('for' and 'against')

b) Use the 'reading for criticism' approach (see page 27)

c) List the consequences that flow from such points or ideas

3 Review recent notes you have taken:

a) What abbreviations can you make?

b) Rewrite your notes using your own 'shorthand' and the 'key word' approach

4 Appraise your approach to note-taking:

a) Establish a notes information base

b) Apply the 'inputs' and 'outputs' approach; make your notes work for you (review page 33)

5 If you have been given the opportunity to choose your research topic, use the following procedures to select an appropriate one:

a) Follow the 'process' approach indicated on page 40

b) Use the 'first thoughts' list as a guide (page 44)

c) Use the focusing approach recommended on page 43

d) Ask yourself the key questions and develop your personal checklist (review page 41)

e) Prepare a research outline using the criteria on page 44 as a guide

Developing writing skills

Rightly or wrongly, writing – whether in the form of an essay, dissertation or exam – is the main method of assessing academic performance. Good writing requires various skills, including the ability to use grammar and punctuation appropriately, to provide a suitable structure, to reason logically and to use evidence effectively. Demonstrating that you can write effectively also provides evidence that you have mastered the learning skills described on page 3.

This chapter highlights the skills and strategies necessary for effective writing and will help you become aware of the problems you may face when trying to improve your writing. It covers:

- punctuation
- problem areas (e.g., active and passive voice)
- sentence and paragraph technique
- structure
- style
- summarising
- the use of evidence.

3.1 Academic writing

The main function of academic writing is to analyse, present ideas, argue effectively, determine consequences and reach conclusions ('the good answer always goes on to say why'). One reason why writing in general requires such great skill is that it is a one-way method of communication. Unlike the spoken word, the writer does not have the benefit of important communication elements such as immediate feedback, confirmation of understanding and aspects of non-verbal behaviour. So skilled writers have to try to anticipate readers' reactions to what has been written:

- Will they understand the terminology?

- Will they accept the ideas, arguments or conclusions?

- Can they follow the structure used?

- What questions might they have (and what is the best way of dealing with these)?

In academic writing you must use particular terms and concepts to prove that you understand them and can use them in an appropriate context, but you should not produce 'flowery' prose or use jargon. Indeed, an intelligent writer is economical in the use of words and follows the golden rule for all writing: communicate to be understood.

Writing is the outcome of a number of academic activities and is closely linked to other skills such as reading, planning, analysing, synthesising and all those outlined on page 3. Table 3.1 provides a brief explanation of some grammatical terms.

Table 3.1 Grammatical terms ▼

Term	Description	Examples
Adjective	describes a noun or pronoun	*red* book, *wide* corridor
Adverb	improves a verb by indicating why/where/when/how action occurs	*neatly* done, *very* clean
Clauses	groups of words with a finite verb (includes adjectives, adverbs, nouns)	the students went quiet *when the exam results went up*
Cliché	an expression that is overused	the final straw (see page 64)
Conjunction	joins or shows the relationship between words and phrases	coursework *and* exams; results are good but not outstanding
Metaphor	a word or phrase that implies a likeness between different things	she is as bright as a button

Noun	name of a person, place or thing	student, college, essay
Pronoun	used to avoid repeating a noun	me, you, they, them, who
Personal pronouns	1st person 2nd person 3rd person	*Singular*　*Plural* I/me　we/us you　you she/he/it/　they/them him/her
Prefix	letters added at the start of a word to modify its meaning (may or may not be hyphenated)	ante-room, intercity
Suffix	letters added at the end of a word to modify its meaning	quietly, policeman
Verb	a 'doing' word	she *went* to college

Effective academic writing involves a number of skills and requires an awareness of various issues, so a personal checklist is a useful aid.

▲
Table 3.1
Grammatical
terms
(contd)

Checklist: academic writing

You should:

- consider the reader

- provide a logical structure

- use evidence and quotations appropriately

- have a good command of grammar, sentence structure and paragraphing technique

- conduct appropriate research

- provide a strong argument

- use an appropriate style

- consider the outcomes and consequences of any points raised.

The following deficiencies are sometimes found in student writing:

- too little or too much punctuation

- lack of general structure

- an inappropriate writing style

- poor sentence and paragraph structure

- confusing the active and passive voice

- ineffective and wrong use of evidence and quotations

- an inability to summarise properly

- clichés and mixed metaphors.

3.2 Punctuation

Because writing is a one-way form of communication (with all the limitations that this imposes), you need to make an extra effort to help the reader understand specific meanings, emphasis and the way you think about particular issues. Punctuation is the main way of doing this. It plays the role in the written word as tone, pauses, inflections and stress on certain words do in the spoken word. For instance, italics or underlining can be used to emphasise certain words in a sentence, thus altering the meaning:

- *I* want you to do this job now.

- I *want* you to do this job now.

- I want *you* to do this job now.

- I want you to do *this* job now.

- I want you to do this job *now*.

Full stop

The full stop indicates the longest pause and marks the end of a sentence (unless it is a question or exclamation). It can also be used in abbreviations and shortened versions of words. A full stop indicates a complete unit of meaning. Although the start of sentences is clearly defined (with a capital letter), when they stop is a matter of whether or not the meaning is complete.

In abbreviations, the full stop is normally used only where the shortened version does not contain the last letters of the word (for example, etc., vol.). Nowadays, full stops are rarely used where the abbreviation contains capital letters (for example, MP, TUC, CBI). However, full stops are sometimes used where lower case letters are included in the abbreviation, for example Dip. Ed. (Diploma in Education).

Comma

Although commas have many uses, they are mainly used to separate a collection of words, phrases or clauses. For example:

- a series of nouns – The corridor was strewn with paint, glass, and papers.

- a series of adjectives – She was an intelligent, diligent and well-liked student.

- a series of verbs or clauses – He studied hard, revised methodically, and successfully completed his examinations.

Another example of the use of a comma is where it highlights an adjectival clause which in itself does not qualify or define. For example:

The students, who studied hard, were successful.

Without commas this sentence would mean that only the students who studied hard were successful; with commas it means that all the students who studied hard were successful. Another important use of the comma, which students often forget, is to separate sentence 'qualifiers' (or 'transition' words) that provide the link between a preceding sentence and the next – for example: accordingly, consequently, however, etc. (such words are also referred to as sentence adverbs).

Semicolon

In terms of strength, the semicolon is halfway between a comma and a full stop. In other words, it indicates a pause longer than a comma but less than a full stop. It can be used in various ways:

- To link sentences that could stand separately, but are closely related (a full stop would get in the way). For example:

  - Social sciences, arts and English students should enrol on Monday; construction, motor vehicle and computer students should enrol on Tuesday; business, management and nursing students should enrol on Wednesday.

- When the second clause expands upon, or explains the first. For example:

  - 'She was overjoyed and speechless; she had passed all her exams with top grades.'

- To highlight contrasts. For example:

  - 'Brian was an extrovert; David was an introvert.'

- When different aspects of the same sentence are referred to, or a sequence of actions is described. For example:

  - His throat was dry; his hands were shaking; the examination was about to begin.

The semicolon is also used when various parts of a list contain commas and using commas as 'separators' would cause confusion. For example:

Candidates should possess a good degree, preferably in economics; a knowledge of computing; and be willing to travel in the UK and overseas, in the course of their work.

Colon

The colon signals a change in meaning which is more sudden than that suggested by the semicolon. The colon usually precedes an example, a list, or an extended quotation. It can also be used before a clause that clarifies or expands upon a previous sentence. For example:

> The computer course was the only one for Mike: he lived and breathed computers, he had relevant qualifications, and it was his chosen career.

Apostrophe

The apostrophe is a punctuation mark that seems to cause particular problems for students. All you need to remember is that it has two main uses:

- To show possession where nouns are concerned. Singular nouns and plural nouns not ending in s have an apostrophe *before* the final s; plural nouns ending in s have an apostrophe *after* the final s. For example:

    - the student's briefcase (singular noun)

    - women's courses (plural noun not ending in s)

    - students' complaints (plural ending in s).

- To replace an absent letter or letters. For example:

    - we're, they're, didn't (one letter absent)

    - won't, we'll, we'd (more than one letter absent).

Question mark

The question mark is used at the end of every sentence where a question is asked in direct speech. It is not used where a question is asked in indirect speech. For example:

- When will we get the exam results? (direct speech)

- She asked when we would get the exam results. (indirect speech.)

Exclamation mark

The exclamation mark is used to register emphasis, alarm, surprise, anger or a sharp comment. For example:

Leave it! Goodbye!

It can also be used to add a note of irony or sarcasm. For example:

I believe you, thousands wouldn't!

Exclamation marks should be used sparingly. Indeed, in academic writing, it is better to try to develop your emphatic skills (how you emphasise things) through the use of language structure.

Quotation marks

Some students put quotation marks (or inverted commas) around almost every word or term they do not understand. Quotation marks have three main uses:

1 To indicate direct speech – for example: 'When are we starting revision?' she said.

2 To highlight quotations – for example: According to Thomas Edison, 'Genius is one per cent inspiration and ninety-nine per cent perspiration.'

3 For names of houses, books, newspapers, plays, etc. – for example: The house on the hill was called 'Glenmartin'. (But note that in many publications the titles of books, newspapers, plays, etc. are set in italics.)

Note also:

- If a question or direct speech has a 'saying' verb in front of it such as states, claims, etc. (as in 2 above), a comma should be used after the verb.

- Using single or double quotation marks is a matter of personal style. (In this book the style is to generally use single quotation marks.) If a quotation contains direct speech within it, double quotation marks should be used for the direct speech (or vice versa). For example:

  - Hermione said, 'We were given some advice about writing style by Samuel Johnson: "Read over your compositions, and wherever you meet with a passage which you think is particularly fine, strike it out."'

- Quotation marks can be used to indicate that you are simply referring to a term rather than using it. For example:

  - 'Law and order' can mean either the legitimate and due process of law, or rule by the mob.

    They can also be used to undermine the accepted use of a term, or to disassociate yourself from the way in which it is used. For example:

  - Fortunately, Mr Black was not in the education service. His view of 'education' was early rising, working students until they dropped and swift punishment.

Hyphen

Unlike the dash, which is used to mark the insertion of a clause, emphasis or a change of thought, the hyphen is used to link words. It does so by helping to attach prefixes to words, to avoid confusion, or to form a compound word from one or more others. For example:

- ex-husband, non-existent, vice-president (attaching prefixes)

- re-emerge

- up-to-date, over-the-top, mother-in-law (forming a compound word)

3.3 Problem areas
Active and passive voice

Using the passive voice often leads to sentences being awkward. As the following examples show, apart from economising on words, the active voice is more direct.

- Passive voice: Anxiety is caused for some students when examination time comes.

- Active voice: Examinations cause anxiety for some students.

Clichés

Using clichés is a sign that the writer may lack original thought. It is also boring and often reduces the sentence to a collection of meaningless phrases. The following are examples of clichés to be avoided at all costs (see how easy it is to fall into the cliché trap!):

- afford an opportunity

- all things considered

- arguably

- as it were

- at this point in time

- auspicious occasion

- barometer of ...

- be that as it may

- blanket coverage

- generally speaking

- give rise to

- hive of activity

'Flowery' language

'Notwithstanding, it is needless to say, that a variable number of those engaged in learned activities perhaps, over a long period of time, in certain circumstances, find themselves at a pecuniary disadvantage.'

A 'flowery' writer is someone who *invariably engages in quite substantial circumlocution* (see the problem?). In plain language, a flowery writer is someone who uses elaborate words, phrases or sentence structure in order to impress. This is a temptation if you are new to academic writing or if you have not written in academic style for some time – you should resist it. The writer of the paragraph above was trying to say:

'Students often find that they don't have enough money.'

Mixed metaphors

Mixed metaphors often occur if you are in the habit of using clichés. For example:

It's as plain as black and white that he's green with envy.

Unfortunately, things can get worse. This happens when the metaphor is linked to the literal (known as a syllepsis) to form a nonsensical sentence:

As soon as he opened his mouth, he put his foot in it.

Tautology

Tautology is repeating what has already been stated in order to imply extra meaning. Not only is the additional word (or words) unnecessary, but being tautologous undermines the academic authority of what has been stated. For example:

Will this report be adequate enough? (The word 'enough' is unnecessary.)

Words to watch

In everyday conversation or reading, most people can understand what is being stated without knowing the exact meaning of every word. There are several reasons for this, including people's existing 'bank' of words, the sentence structure used and the context. However, in academic writing it is essential that the writer understands the precise meaning of the words used.

The following are examples of the many words that can cause confusion to writers when they are used in the written context.

a, an, and

A is used before words beginning with a sounded consonant (regardless of spelling) and *an* before words that begin with a sounded vowel. Note that *a* is used where an initial *h* is pronounced (a hall) and *an* where the *h* is silent (an hour). Although it should not be overused, *and* can be used to start a sentence.

Affect, effect

Affect is a verb meaning to change, alter or influence (lack of education can affect your future). *Effect* when used as a verb refers to a consequence, aftermath or conclusion (the change in staffing was effected by making James the head of department). *Effect* can also be used as a noun (the effect of Jane's thorough revision was excellent exam results).

Alternate, alternative

These two words are often confused. *Alternate* means to occur, or cause to occur by turns ('the seasons alternate'). *Alternative* implies the possibility of choice ('the course could be completed in one year full-time, or alternatively, two years part-time').

Allusion, illusion

An *allusion* is a passing or indirect reference. An *illusion* is a false or deceptive appearance of reality.

Amid, among

Amid means 'in the middle of'; *among* means in the group, class or number of.

Although, though

These are conjunctions and mean, 'despite the fact that'. As conjunctions they are usually interchangeable ('she accepted the college course although/though it was not her first choice').

Anybody, anyone

Anybody and *anyone* are pronouns and are interchangeable. They are usually one word except where the emphasis is on the second part ('he received several offers from colleges, but any one of them would have been acceptable'). Both words are singular, and should be followed by singular pronouns and verbs.

Appendix, appendices

Appendices is the plural of the noun appendix. Another plural, *appendixes*, also exists, but it is not often used.

Besides

Using *besides* to mean *alternately* is wrong. Besides means 'in addition to' or 'also'. 'There must be additional reasons for his poor exam performance *besides* lack of technique' is an example of *incorrect* use. The use of 'other than' rather than besides would have been more appropriate.

Can, may

Can is a verb and means what is possible ('Can I join your study group?'). *May* is also a verb, but it applies to what is permissible ('May I change my tutorial group?').

Comparatively, compare to, compare with

Comparatively means relatively, and its use should be avoided unless a comparison is being made or clearly implied. *Compare to* should be used when things are similar to each other ('Shall I compare thee to a summer's day?'). *Compare with* should be used when the differences are stressed (David compared this year's results with those from last year).

Continual, continuous

Continual means recurring frequently, particularly at regular intervals. *Continuous* means unceasing, without break or interruption.

Define, definitive

Define is a verb meaning to state precisely. *Definitive* is an adjective that means serving as a reference point (the definitive guide to gap year working).

Dependant, dependent

When used as an adjective the spelling is *dependent*, which means reliant, or depending on a person for support ('admission to the course was dependent upon good grades'). When used as a noun the spelling is *dependant*, which refers to a person who is reliant or depending on another ('before sentencing, the judge asked if the accused had any dependants').

Despite, in spite of

Both are completely interchangeable, but *despite* is often preferred for conciseness.

Distinct, distinctive

Although these two adjectives are not interchangeable, they are often confused. *Distinct* means definite, easily recognisable or distinguishable ('there's a distinct smell of burning'). *Distinctive* means characteristic, serving or tending to distinguish ('she had a distinctive manner').

e.g., i.e.

These two abbreviations are often confused. *e.g.* is short for 'exampli gratia' and means 'for example' *i.e.* stands for 'id est' and means that's it/that is.

he, she

There are several ways round the problem of whether or not to use *he* or *she* as personal pronouns when the gender of the individual is not specified:

- Use he or she; his, her or he/she (but this can be awkward).

- Restructure the sentence to make the subject plural – for example: instead of 'The student must pay his or her enrolment fee before the course commences', you can write 'Students must pay enrolment fees before the course commences'.

- Use they, them, their(s) as singular pronouns.

I, me

I (subject pronoun) and *me* (object pronoun) are often confused, particularly in informal speech. Technically, *I* should be used before verbs and *me* after verbs and prepositions. A more useful method is to mentally shorten the sentence. For example, shortening the following sentence from 'The first-year students asked Brian and I/me to join their study group' to 'the first-year students asked I/me ...' indicates that *me* is the appropriate words to use.

In, into, in to

In usually implies a certain place or fixed position ('no smoking in the lecture theatre'). *Into* is also a preposition, but it often indicates movement ('she drove into the car park'). As prepositions, both *in* and *into* can be interchangeable at times ('she put the book in/into her briefcase'). *In to* as two words is correct when 'in' is an adverb ('he went in to rest').

Militate, mitigate

Militate (verb) is often used with against (preposition) and means to have influence or effect ('although the student protested his innocence, the evidence militated against him'). *Mitigate* is also a verb and means to make or become less harsh ('the exam board's finding did little to mitigate the student's disappointment').

of (have), off (from)

The preposition *of* is often mistakenly used instead of the verb *have* ('the students should have [not of] taken better notes'). It is considered wrong by some people to use the preposition *off* instead of *from* to demonstrate acquisition ('the tutor took the radio from [not off] the student').

Oral, verbal

Oral can be used only in connection with the spoken word; *verbal* can be used in both spoken and written contexts.

Shall, will

The general and traditional rule is that to express the future, *shall* is used in the first person and *will* in the second and third persons. To express intention, determination and so on, *will* should be used in the first person and *shall* in the second and third persons. The use of *shall* or *will* is also determined by such things as regional influences and the level or intensity of expression intended.

That, which

The distinction between these two words is associated with the difference between defining and non-defining clauses. A defining clause is one that is necessary for the sentence to be sensible and logical, for example 'The college that had specialist courses was popular'. With no commas before or after the phrase 'that had specialist courses', the implication is that the college was popular because it had specialist courses.

However, in the sentence 'The college, which had specialist courses, was popular' the phrase 'which had specialist courses' has been rendered almost incidental with commas placed before and after it. In other words, if the phrase between commas was placed in brackets or deleted, it would make no difference to the logic of the sentence, i.e. the college was popular.

3.4 Sentence structure and paragraph technique

The section on punctuation has included many references to sentences. However, the sentence is so important that this section will look exclusively at the various types of sentence construction and some common problems.

It is useful to remember that the basic sentence is composed of three main elements. For example, 'Mike lifted the pen' consists of:

- a subject (Mike)

- a verb (lifted)

- an object or predicate (the pen).

Many of the mistakes that students make regarding sentence structure arise because they either ignore the basic principles of sentence construction outlined above (subject, verb, object), or leave out one of these elements. Poor sentence construction can also arise when all the elements are present but the linkage between them is defective.

Sentence construction

Consider the following example of poor sentence construction:

> The substantial increase in student debt, the high numbers who have, or are seeking part-time employment, and the increasing number requiring professional counselling are outward signs of the huge pressure on students, staff and resources within higher education institutions – fewer career opportunities adds to the pressure on students and worsens the whole situation. Increased stress-related illness rates among lecturing staff is further evidence of the problems caused by the phenomenal increase in student numbers.

Apart from the fact that improved punctuation and grammar could help the reader, the apparent cause of all the problems is left to the last sentence (the increase in student numbers). Although the 'cause and effect' approach cannot be applied in all cases and to all parts of a sentence, in this instance, using such an approach can improve matters:

> The phenomenal increase in higher education students has led to a number of problems: large numbers of students already have, or are seeking, part-time employment; there is a substantial increase in student debt; and more and more students require professional counselling. These problems, along with increased stress-related illness rates among lecturing staff, are held to be outward signs of these pressures on staff and resources. The fact that currently, there are fewer career opportunities, adds to the pressure on students and the situation in general.

Unity

A sentence is a unit of expression, and although it may contain more than one fact, all the facts must be related to the main idea or theme. Consider the following example of poor sentence unity:

> The students were welcomed by their tutor who outlined the course, some had their own cars, and some came by bus.

Topic sentences

A topic sentence first (TSF) approach puts the main idea at the beginning and the supporting, less important details at the end (the deductive pattern). The problem is that the writer is tempted to overload the sentence with fact after fact until the sentence has lost its unity. For example:

> The changes to the curriculum seem to be working, this is just as well, since students have been failing during the last two academic years, although the appointment of a new course team leader has increased the motivation of the tutors concerned, and this of course has been reflected in even more curriculum innovations.

However, used with good sense, the TSF approach has the advantage of placing the main idea first in the reader's mind, and then adding the supporting detail:

> *Study skills are vital if students are to succeed.* This involves real skill development in such areas as: planning and organising; how to use a library; reading academic texts; note-taking; writing; and revision and examination techniques. Such skills should be taught on all first-year courses, and especially access courses.

In contrast, the topic sentence last approach (TSL) uses a build-up effect to postpone the main idea to the end, thereby stimulating the reader's curiosity. You only understand when you have read the whole sentence:

> After months of negotiation, goodwill on all sides, and some amendments, the new working practices were finally adopted by the workforce.

The problem with the TSL is that the writer can get carried away with details, leaving the reader struggling to link them to the main idea (when it finally arrives).

Positive and negative sentences

A positive sentence is one that is constructive, emphasising what can be achieved; a negative sentence is, of course, the opposite. So positive sentences generally give more information and appear more acceptable. For example:

- The student's essay is late. (negative)

- The student's essay will be presented tomorrow. (positive)

Emphasis in a sentence

Although there are several ways to emphasise particular points in a sentence, these techniques should be used sparingly.

1 **Repeating certain words or phrases** – 'music was her hobby, her future, her life'.

2 **Contrasting** – using opposite statements to produce a contrasting effect:

'Where life is concerned, unless you understand where you are coming from, you will never understand where you are going.'

3 **Using transition words** – 'joining' words such as 'not only ... but also':

'She hoped that students would not only learn from the course, but also enjoy it.'

4 **Using particular constructions** – such as 'it was':

'My students did very well this year.'

'It was my students who did very well this year.'

5 **Complementary structure** – giving two or more parts of the same sentence a similar structure to highlight a certain point:

'It was not by giving them the answers, but by giving them the means to obtain the answers, that the teacher developed their problem-solving ability.'

6 **Changing word order** – altering the word order to produce a more positive or dramatic effect:

'He managed to pass the exam although he was a weak student.'

'Although he was a weak student he managed to pass the exam.'

Paragraphs

The two main characteristics of a good paragraph are unity and logical order. Everything in a paragraph should be related to the specific idea or theme and be capable of being summed up in a single sentence. All other sentences should develop that topic sentence (for example, the first sentence in this paragraph). Sentences should follow each other in logical sequence, thus leading the reader from one thought to the next.

There are two types of paragraph patterns:

- Deductive (topic sentence first) – quickly reveals the subject of the paragraph; makes for easy reading.

- Inductive (topic sentence last) – provides a build-up effect; useful when persuasion needed.

Techniques	Examples
Listing	The lecturer said that there were three main reasons for ...
Examples	Students will not enjoy a comfortable life if they do not submit work on time.
Cause and effect	If students write carelessly, then tutors will have difficulty in reading their work.
Comparison and contrast	In my view, multiple-choice exams have both advantages and disadvantages.
Definition	By education I mean how people learn, as well as what they learn.
Question and answer	The question is, will the students work hard? If so, they will reap the rewards.
Logical order	In the first two paragraphs introducing the section on paragraphs, the topic sentence is placed at the beginning.

▲
*Table 3.2
Paragraph
techniques*

Although the importance of grammar, punctuation and sentence structure cannot be overstated, paragraphs provide the 'milestones' in any written piece. They are the steps along the road of the argument or thesis.

Long paragraphs should be avoided. Not only are they difficult to read, but they can also be an indication that the writer is not too clear about the argument or thesis. Paragraphs are important because they can:

● introduce the main ideas or argument

● compare and contrast opposing arguments

● allow for pauses (to take in ideas)

● develop points already made

● signal a change in direction

● lead to summaries or conclusions.

3.5 Structure

Structuring written work entails linking arguments, opinions or the elements of an argument so that they appear logical, effective and compelling. The structure of essays, reports and dissertations is dealt with in Chapters 4 and 5.

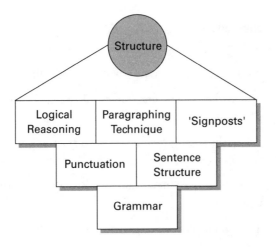

Figure 3.1
Building blocks
of structure

Focus points: structure

An ineffective piece of writing often contains some of the following:

- a complete lack of structure

- no introduction

- too many ideas and/or irrelevant information

- paragraphs that are too long and/or contain too many separate ideas

- the writer frequently strays from the point

- no clear distinction between opposing arguments

- no real conclusion, or the conclusion reached does not follow the evidence provided

- the structure does not comply with the instructions given (e.g., 'discuss', 'evaluate', 'analyse', etc.) or the task set

- there are no 'signposts' to guide the reader through the various stages of the argument or comparative analysis

- the summary or conclusion simply repeats what has already been stated, with little or no additional comment.

Key questions
Ask yourself:

- Is the topic or theme clear? (good introduction)

- What are the main points? (topic sentences and effective paragraphs)

- Is there logical progression? (are the main points sensibly ordered?)

- Does the argument 'flow'? (appropriate linking words and phrases)

- Is the argument convincing? (writing skill, style and evidence)

- Does the argument go beyond the material used? (are the wider implications considered?)

The *topic sentence* is a key element in the structure and, as noted, it can be placed either at the start of the paragraph or at the end. Other sentences must be related to, and develop, the main idea or point included in the topic sentence. Paragraph length is also important, and although this depends upon the project, a paragraph length of approximately 100 words helps the reader to concentrate on the key points.

Transitions

Transitions (or linking words) are the link in the paragraph 'chain'. They enable the reader conveniently to identify emphasis, the development of points and changes in direction. Here are some examples of the many transitions, linking or 'indicator' words which are necessary for the logical flow of ideas or key points:

- *In contrast*, Jones maintains

- *However*, Scott (2003) contends (refutes or indicates contrasting/alternative position)

- *Notwithstanding*, it must be remembered (something else to consider)

- *Despite this fact/although it has been stated* (concedes a point, but reminds us that there is another side to the story)

- *Furthermore, in addition, indeed, moreover* etc. (signals that there is going to be more of the same)

- *Consequently, accordingly, therefore, thus, hence* etc. (begins to conclude)

And there are more:

- *Before considering* A it is important to briefly consider B

- *Having dealt with* X we must proceed to Y

- *While considering* A, it must also be borne in mind

- *As a result*, it can be seen that...

- Phillips *maintains/claims/asserts/expounds that...*

- *It can be argued that*

- *It might be said that*

- *The use of the term*

   Using transitions is an important writing technique, and mastering the use of them is crucial to providing an effective structure.

3.6 Reasoning

Whether thinking, talking or writing, providing a logical structure is of fundamental importance. In logic, there are two main methods of reasoning:

- Deductive – the deductive method (also referred to as vertical thinking) proceeds from the general statement (thesis) to the specific details, example, or case.

- Inductive – the inductive approach proceeds from the particular details, example or case to the general statement based upon them. It is founded on concrete matters – experience and observation – rather than on theory.

Although conclusions reached by induction can have a high standard of accuracy, they do not have the same degree of certainty as those arrived at through deduction.

Inductive reasoning

Specific → The employer set up procedures to ensure more interesting work, more freedom, skill development and team pride (specific details)

General → This resulted in reduced absenteeism, fewer staff leaving, improved quality and higher productivity (line of argument/thesis)

Deductive reasoning

General → Research indicates that redesigning jobs improves morale, product quality and job satisfaction (line of argument/thesis)

Specific → Workers are allowed to rotate between tasks, plan their work, and set goals and targets (specific details)

Other reasoning strategies

Cause and effect

This was referred to in the section on paragraph technique. It is based on the belief that an effect is directly attributed to a specific cause. This method of reasoning is best checked by determining whether:

- the cause in question could be the effect of some other cause

- both the cause and the effect could be a result of separate events (i.e. not directly linked at all).

Perfect and imperfect logic

A syllogism is a true logical process composed of the following:

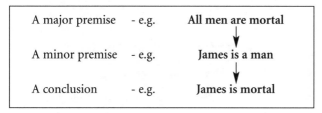

A major premise	- e.g.	**All men are mortal**
A minor premise	- e.g.	**James is a man**
A conclusion	- e.g.	**James is mortal**

On some occasions, mistakes or fallacies occur when the conclusion, although logically correct in relation to the premises, is in itself false. For example:

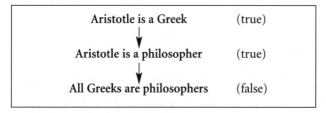

Aristotle is a Greek (true)

Aristotle is a philosopher (true)

All Greeks are philosophers (false)

Whichever method of reasoning is chosen, one important rule must be observed: the conclusion must always follow from the facts and evidence presented.

Checklist: structure
Think

- What needs to be said? (main topic or theme)

- What are the main points? (argument structure)

- What order should they take? (prioritise)

- What position will be taken? (e.g., for, against etc.)

- What does the instruction entail? (e.g., discuss, evaluate etc.)

- How will I generate ideas? (e.g., pattern notes)

- What reasoning strategy? (e.g., inductive, deductive)

Plan

- What is the best way to say it? (sequence and development)

- What are the counter arguments? (objectivity)

- How many paragraphs? (clarity and conciseness)

- What knowledge is required? (research)

- Is there a distinct beginning, middle and end? (a basic structure)

- Are there relevant notes? (build on existing knowledge)

- Is all the material relevant? (avoid straying off the point)

- Is the draft outline adequate? (problem identification)

Write

- Is the introduction adequate? ('setting the scene')

- Are key terms defined? (demonstrating understanding)

- Are the topic sentences clear? (making key points)

- Is the case developed logically and coherently? (academic thoroughness)

- Are there sufficient transitions? (helping 'flow')

- Is the case presented objectively? (strengthens the argument)

- Has the evidence been used convincingly? (vital for acceptance)

- Does the conclusion go beyond simple restatement? (transcending the obvious)

3.7 Style

This section on writing style comes after the one on
structure because, although they are closely linked,
structure is more important than style. Structure is
the 'nuts and bolts' of writing, and only when you have
mastered it sufficiently should you start to develop a
sense of style.

Style is important because it enables you to do more than
simply report the various viewpoints and positions held. If
you have a command of style, you will be able to go beyond
simple account-giving, and not merely reflect the argument
but participate in it as well.

With practice, most students can use evidence and state a
case to a good standard. However, it is above-average
students who produce compelling comments and
convincing arguments, and who effectively challenge
existing theories and firmly held beliefs. They can only do
this if they are skilled at persuasion.

A well-developed style is an essential component of
persuasion, but it is not the only one. Style without incisive
analysis, effective structure, logical argument and
convincing use of evidence will fail to persuade. This is
particularly apparent when a writer, faced with a lack of
evidence, tries to mask a personal belief or opinion as a fact.
This misuse of style often entails the use of 'convincers' –
words that the writer hopes will lend some authority or
substance to the contention masquerading as a fact.
Examples of convincers are: obviously, undeniable (fact),
self-evident (when it is not), and quite apparent (again,
when it is not)

But what is style? In many contexts it is a
characteristic manner of expression. In the case of
writing, style is composed of a number of elements (see
Figure 3.2).

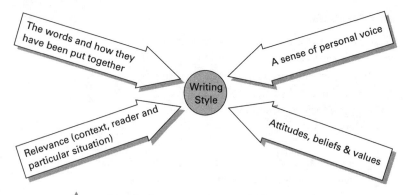

Figure 3.2
Writing style

Developing your writing style is a continuous process, and your style will change over time. Style arises partly from appraising the views of others and partly as a result of the development of your own point of view across a range of issues.

Words

Much of the material in this chapter is relevant to writing style. Emphasis in a sentence (page 74), for instance, illustrates the way in which words can be used and changed around to give a different meaning or emphasis. Famous orators often use a play-on-words technique to get key points across in a vivid and dramatic way.

Many of Winston Churchill's speeches contain illustrations of how simple words can be used in a particular sequence to good effect. His speech after El Alamein (1942) is a good example of a play on words:

> *This is not the end. It is not even the beginning of the end. But it is perhaps, the end of the beginning.*

Another of his famous speeches (August 1940) contains an example of what is known as 'the rule of three':

> *Never in the field of human conflict has so much been owed by so many to so few.*

Although the word *so* is repeated three times, it is the addition of *much*, *many* and *few*, in a specific sequence, that creates the dramatic effect.

Another famous example of the repetition of a key word or phrase is in a speech by Martin Luther King (August 1963). The phrase 'let freedom ring' was used a number of times in the latter part of King's speech. But it was another phrase, repeated again and again at strategic intervals throughout his address, which made it one of the most memorable speeches with regard to human aspiration. The phrase was, 'I have a dream'. The following is an extract from King's speech:

> *I have a dream that one day this Nation will rise up and live out the true meaning of its creeds – 'we hold these truths to be self-evident that all men are created equal'.*

> *I have a dream that one day on the red hills of Georgia the sons of slaves and the sons of former slaveowners will be able to sit down together at the table of brotherhood. I have a dream that one day even the state of Mississippi, sweltering with the heat of injustice, sweltering with the heat of oppression, will be transformed into an oasis of freedom and justice.*

> *I have a dream today ...*

Many speech-making techniques can, if used sensitively and sparingly, enhance a written piece of work. For instance, a social science student who has a fondness for finishing with a flourish might wish to end an essay on the purpose of education by using the rule of three:

> In the final analysis, education must meet the development needs of the individual as well as the

functional needs of society. Education, then, must be a process of developing self-analysis, self-realisation and self-fulfilment.

A social science student asked to explore the origin of power in society in an essay could, having examined the various theories, make the following point:

> Whereas for Marx, power in society arose from *the ownership of the means of production*, for Weber, power in society arose from the *ownership* of *the means of administration*.

This phrase not only contains a subtle contrast of words, but also concisely defines the opposing views. Care must be taken with these aspects of style. The overuse of techniques like this can reduce written work to a collection of clichés.

The build-up approach

While it is generally good practice to keep things simple, there are times when a more elaborate approach is required. The build-up approach is an example of how words are linked together in a developmental way to add emphasis or a sense of atmosphere:

> The students were subdued, their usual humour and banter was absent. The lecturer surveyed the room. He sympathised, but had to maintain his professional role. 'You may write your name and candidate number, but do not turn over the paper until I say so. You may begin now.'

A key element of the build-up effect is that each succeeding sentence acts like a jigsaw piece or frame of a film, thus contributing to the complete picture.

Personal voice

A sense of personal voice is an aspect of writing style that is difficult to explain. It is an individual quality or feeling created by the distinctive way in which the piece is written. It also makes a statement about the writer's attitudes, beliefs, values, strength of commitment, fluency and persuasive ability.

To some extent, a sense of personal voice implies ownership of a written piece since it is more than just repeating the conventional wisdom about a particular issue or issues.

Relevancy

Another definition of style is 'to adapt or make suitable for'. Applied to writing, this implies appropriateness in terms of content, reader and the particular situation. Before including any element of content, you should ask these key questions:

- *Why* include it? (relevancy)

- *How* is it linked? (order)

- *What* will the reader think? (impact)

   Consideration of the reader is essential and the structure checklist (see page 81) is a useful guide. For academic purposes, the main reader is usually a tutor, who will have certain expectations in terms of an adequate response to the task set, specific grading criteria and perhaps a preferred style. For instance, tutors often prefer essays to be written in the third person (see page 89).

Persuasion

Unlike an orator, who can use a variety of verbal and non-verbal techniques, a writer is confined by the one-way nature of the written word. Nevertheless, there are some approaches to aid persuasive writing.

1 Establish rapport and credibility:

- demonstrate competence (writing ability)

- clearly and concisely outline the issue or issues

- confirm a sense of personal voice

- recognise or concede one or more aspects of the opposing argument (but then subtly undermine them).

2 Use effective reasoning:

- give logical and acceptable reasons for your point of view

- answer the question *why*? (state your case)

- anticipate and allow for negative response or disbelief (e.g., 'whilst Andrews (1990) is correct in stating ... Scott and Johnson (1991) draw attention to the fact that ...')

- use evidence selectively (but carefully, or you could be accused of bias).

3 Use effective writing techniques:

- plan structure and style carefully (would you be convinced?)

- use short sentences

- use the active rather than the passive voice (review page 64)

- emphasise or repeat key points

- control sentence rhythm to build up pace

- finish with a concise but powerful argument.

Choosing tense: first, second or third?

Whether you write in the first, second or third person (or tense) depends upon a number of factors, but before considering these it is important to distinguish between them:

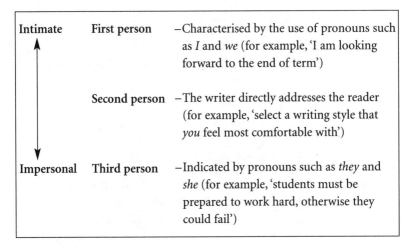

Intimate	First person	–Characterised by the use of pronouns such as *I* and *we* (for example, 'I am looking forward to the end of term')
↑	Second person	–The writer directly addresses the reader (for example, 'select a writing style that *you* feel most comfortable with')
↓ Impersonal	Third person	–Indicated by pronouns such as *they* and *she* (for example, 'students must be prepared to work hard, otherwise they could fail')

3.8 Summarising

The ability to summarise effectively is not just important in academic work, it is also a crucial business and life skill. Being able to quickly grasp the main points of a verbal statement or written passage is an invaluable communication skill. Although summarising is associated with other activities such as note-taking, it takes on an added emphasis when written work is being prepared, particularly when the work is being formally assessed. As well as providing evidence that you can work to a deadline ('In 1,500 words, examine the claim that ...'), summarising effectively is proof that you have mastered essential academic skills, skills such as:

- **Perception** – reading perceptively.

- **Comprehension** – understanding the main points of a statement, passage, argument, or theory.

- **Analysis** – analysing and classifying information.

- **Evaluation** – evaluating, prioritising and selecting the relevant facts.

- **Fluency** – using words that convey the tone of the original.

Focus points: summarising

Potential problems include:

- failure to grasp the main facts in a variety of contexts (e.g., research)

- failure to meet remits and deadlines

- straying from the main points in essays etc.

- poorer performance in examinations.

The various terms associated with summarising are sometimes confused. For example, précis is often used instead of summary, but the words have different meanings. The main terms relating to the process of summarising are defined in the box.

Précis	a faithful reduction of an original passage. The aim of a précis is to reproduce the tone of the original as well as the main facts. Where possible, the original wording is maintained (but in abbreviated form).
Summary	a more selective reproduction of a statement, article or passage. The facts are usually being summarised for a particular purpose. The person making the summary often uses their own words to link the relevant facts.
Abstract	a short summary of a passage, containing all the salient points but no details. The length of the abstract is determined by the purpose for which it is being made.

Summaries are usually written in the same tense as the original. The following guidelines may help:

- Avoid personal pronouns.

- Use reported speech if the passage has been written in the first person.

- Use reported speech if a quotation in direct speech has been used.

The flow chart in Figure 3.3 illustrates the main stages in the summary process, but there are some other factors to remember:

- Read the article, passage or item carefully, look for:

  - the general meaning

  - how individual words or phrases are used (sentence structure)

  - the development of the piece and its overall structure (paragraph structure).

- If possible, use the topic sentence approach (page 73) to note the main points.

- Check the selected points against the original, are they relevant and comprehensive enough?

- Devise a new heading if appropriate.

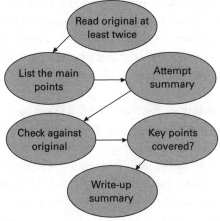

*Figure 3.3
The process of
summarising*

Note: If you are unable to continue with a specific stage, reread and amend accordingly.

Summarising in action

The exercise is to summarise the passage in the box.

> Although in the old days you just had to soldier on where exam stress was concerned, it is now recognised as a serious health hazard.
>
> While many universities and colleges now offer a range of support services (advice sheets, tutorials and counselling), a number of students still suffer from serious exam-related stress. These students are often referred to psychologists.
>
> Dr Mike Paterson is a clinical psychologist who specialises in exam-related stress and is a consultant to a number of health authorities and universities. Dr Paterson often finds that the acute stress can be related to certain areas such as the cumulative effects of day-to-day studying; the stress of intense revision; or sitting the exam itself.
>
> Dr Paterson and his colleagues use a number of techniques, depending upon the particular problem. For example, some students cannot even bear to look at an exam paper without feeling extremely anxious. The technique here is to get the student, over a period of time, to become familiar with exam papers and respective answer strategies.
>
> Practice exams are another tried and tested method for lowering exam stress. Students are taught to work out 'answer plans' for each question and develop time-management strategies. Allocating time appropriately among the various questions helps prevent the situation where students get to the last question and simply 'run out of steam'.

Despite the fact that some students leave revision to the last minute (thus adding to an already stressful situation), Dr Paterson finds that many are simply overwhelmed by the nature of revision itself. Indeed, it is often the dedicated student that falls prey to studying for unrealistically long time periods. Dr Paterson states that it is not unusual for some students to study for 50–60 hours per week. Once again, Dr Paterson and his colleagues work with individual students to draft a realistic revision table that allows for recreation and relaxation.

The key to avoiding the acute stress associated with academic examinations is to have an overall plan of action and think positively – for example, 'I am a good student, I have worked hard, there is no reason why I should not do well'.

357 words

First, you should identify the key points:

1 Exam stress is now recognised as a serious health hazard.

2 A range of support services is available, including referral to a psychologist.

3 According to Dr Mike Paterson (a specialist in exam-related stress), acute stress can be related to certain areas such as day-to-day studying; the stress of intensive revision; or sitting the exam itself.

4 Techniques to counteract stress include: over time, helping the student to be less fearful of exam papers; practice exams; and time-management strategies.

5 It is important that students have a realistic timetable that allows for relaxation; have an overall plan of action; and think positively – for example, 'I am a good student,

I have studied hard, there is no reason why I should not do well'.

Once they have been identified, they can be presented in paragraph form (see box).

Exam stress is now recognised as a serious health hazard. According to Dr Mike Paterson (a specialist in exam-related stress), acute stress can be related to certain areas such as day-to-day studying; the stress of intensive revision; or sitting the exam itself.

However, a range of support services is available including referral to a psychologist. Techniques to counteract stress also include: over time, helping the student to be less fearful of exam papers; practice exams; and time management strategies.

It is vitally important that students have a realistic timetable that allows for relaxation; have an overall plan of action; and think positively – for example, 'I am a good student, I have studied hard, there is no reason why I should not do well'.

123 words

Checklist: summarising

- Be concise: state the main points clearly and leave out unnecessary details.

- Restructure: reduce sentences by using key words; delete phrases or sentences that simply elaborate or repeat a main point.

- Keep it simple: express ideas in plain and simple language. Omit illustrations, comparisons and contrasts where possible.

- Be impartial: don't edit out points you disagree with. It is essential to maintain the tone and balance of the original.

3.9 Providing the evidence

Producing a strong argument involves:

- establishing the facts clearly and logically

- making sound contentions (points made in argument)

- providing alternative lines of thought

- bettering the opposing argument

- offering conclusions, and above all providing the evidence.

Reference to the works of others may be made for a number of reasons. For example, the work concerned may have played a part in shaping your thoughts about a particular issue, supported your views on a specific matter, or simply illustrated an opposite viewpoint. It is not enough simply to cite the works of others, there must be acceptable reasons why they have been used. These may include the particular way in which the work cited clarified the issues involved or enabled you to criticise the opposing line of thought.

Quotations

One of the most common ways of referring to the works of others is quotation, which can be used to:

- provide evidence for your point of view

- clarify or express an idea, concept or thought concisely

- aid analysis of the quotation itself.

There are two main types of quotation: direct quotation, where the writer's actual words are used; and indirect quotation, where the writer's words are paraphrased in your own words. An indirect quotation helps you to clarify your understanding of the quotation because you have to think about what the writer was saying and then express it yourself. Although quotations can be a great aid to effective argument and academic writing in general, care must be taken with respect to:

- quoting out of context

- plagiarism

- using too many quotes.

The use of too many quotes not only reduces the work to a collection of clichés or phrases, it also provides evidence that the writer lacks original thought and analytical skill. Clear differences might also appear with regard to sentence structure and writing style. Most importantly, it could lead to the writer being accused of simply copying someone else's work. Presenting someone else's thoughts and writings as your own is known as *plagiarism*.

It is difficult to express the thoughts and concepts of other writers, particularly when they coincide with your own. So you need to be careful when paraphrasing. You should also clearly indicate when an original source is being used.

Even where the exact words are used, you could be accused of using the quotation out of context. Ellipsis (...) can be used to indicate that the words you have quoted are extracted from a much longer piece of work. However, as the following extract illustrates, even the use of ellipsis does not prevent the selective use of certain words to convey a completely different meaning:

> *Brown (1993) highlights the lack of coherence with respect to study skills teaching in the UK, he refers to, '... the absence of any national programme of curriculum development with regard to study skills'.*

This extract carefully omits the following sentence, which would have provided a more balanced account:

> *However, in spite of the lack of national co-*
> *ordination, significant development has taken place.*

Focus points: using quotations

- Clearly acknowledge the writer, e.g., Jones (1994).

- Use quotation marks.

- Highlight long quotations by indenting.

- Use spacing (e.g., double space from the last line of a long quote).

- Select words which give a fair representation of the other writer's views.

- Punctuate with ellipsis (...) where necessary.

- Use footnotes if relevant.

Checklist: using quotations

Before including a quotation, ask yourself:

- **Why?** (rationale) Is the quote really necessary?

- **Who?** (original thought) Decide what you want to say (either before the quote or after it)

- **How?** (analysis) How can the quote be best used? (e.g., to undermine the opposing viewpoint)

- **What?** (evidence) What writer or writers' views coincide with yours? (why?)

- **When?** (structure) When in the text is the most appropriate place for the quote?

- **Where?** (verification) Where in the cited text does the quotation appear? (e.g., page number.)

References

References are used to:

- indicate the source of a quotation

- document or validate the source used

- refer to another part of your written text.

There are two main referencing techniques: adjacent referencing and numerical referencing.

Adjacent referencing aids the flow of the text and can be used with footnotes or notes at the end of the text (endnotes). The Harvard method is the most common way of making adjacent references, and the following points should be noted:

- Whenever references are made certain details must be given, for example Scott (1999: p. 64), or, ...some writers agree with this point (Scott, 1999: 64). (Whether required to do so or not, it is good practice to give page numbers.)

- If the writer's name occurs naturally or repeatedly in the text, the year of publication should be given in brackets.

- Where the writer has published more than one work in the same year, this should be indicated alphabetically, for example (2001 a).

- Where there is dual authorship, both surnames should be used, for example (Scott & Brown 2004).

- If there are more than two authors, the surname of the first author is used followed by the term et al, e.g. (Brown et al 2005).

- Where the writer cannot be identified, the term anon is used. For example, 'This fact was realised as far back as the 18th century, when it was stated (anon), '...' .'

Numerical referencing involves the use of numerals, either as superscripts – Scott[1] – or in parenthesis – Scott [1]. Explanations of such references can be given as footnotes, at the end of a chapter, or in the bibliography.

Writing a bibliography

A bibliography is an alphabetical list of all the sources used in the preparation of an assignment, whether as a written piece or not. Bibliographies are usually placed at the end of a written text, but they can also be a self-contained work in themselves, providing a comprehensive list of works on a given subject.

You should give as much information as possible so that the sources used can be located easily if required. The Harvard system is the most common method used in bibliographies. The following is an illustration of how it applies to a book:

- author's surname, followed by their initials or first names

- date of publication

- title of book (underlined, or in printed books and journals, in italics)

- place of publication (if possible)

- name of publisher.

Example

One author

Hannigan, T. (2002) *Management Concepts and Practices* (3rd edition), Financial Times/Prentice Hall

Two authors

Robbins, S.P. and Coulter, M. (2002) *Management* (7th edition), New Jersey, Financial Times/Prentice Hall

In an edited book

Bracken, P. (2000) 'Women in the British Army', in H. Strachen (ed.), *The British Army, Manpower and Society into the Twenty-first Century*, Frank Cass Publishers

---

The method for journals is the same, but the volume and issue numbers are given as well. When referring to a website, it is a good idea to include the date when you accessed it, in case it is no longer in existence.

Example

Journal

Williams, M. 'Why is Cornwall Poor? Poverty and In-Migration Since the 1960s', *Contemporary British History*, vol. 17 (3), autumn, 2003

From the internet

Kennedy, J. Learning to Learn (15 February 2005), at/from *www.studymates.co.uk* (accessed 3 March 2005)

Some abbreviations commonly used in references are listed in Table 3.3.

Table 3.3 Aids to referencing ▶

Abbreviation	Meaning
app.	appendix
ibid (ibidem)	in the same work
circa	around a certain date
loc. cit. (loco citato)	in the same place (already cited)
ed./eds	editor(s)
op. cit. (opere citato)	in a work recently cited
et al (et alii)	and others (for several authors)
viz. (videlicet)	namely

Focus points: references

- The absence of references implies that little or no research has been conducted.

- Keep direct quotes to a minimum.

- Just as photocopies are no substitute for understanding, references must not be used as a substitute for your own thoughts or ideas.

- Sentences containing the paraphrased comments of others must always be grammatical.

- If something is added to a reference or quotation (perhaps to clarify), the addition must be enclosed in square brackets. For example, 'Smith's views [about study skills] has caused some consternation'.

- Mistakes in the original text must be repeated when quoting. The word [sic] in square brackets is used to indicate this.

- Always acknowledge sources.

Summary

- Because writing is a one-way method of communication, it requires great skill.

- The written word has a permanence that the spoken word lacks, so mistakes in terms of grammar, incoherence, lack of clarity and inconsistency linger and are magnified.

- Academic writing is not a discrete activity. It is linked to activities such as researching, planning, analysing and synthesising.

- Effective academic writing involves considering the reader, conducting appropriate research, using evidence and providing a logical structure.

- Writing style is very important and its development is a continuous process. It is composed of a number of elements:

  - appraising the views of others

  - the development of your own point of view on a particular subject

  - the development of your thinking.

- The ability to summarise effectively is not just an important writing skill, it is also an essential business and life skill.

- Providing the evidence for statements, key points and contentions is crucial for effective academic writing. Failure to provide such evidence in terms of quotations and references could result in penalties and/or accusations of plagiarism.

Tutorial

1 Use extracts from your written work to determine whether you have:

   a) used the topic sentence approach (page 73)

   b) added increased interest by using techniques such as repetition, contrast, complementary structure and so on (page 74)

   c) used a variety of paragraphing techniques (page 75).

2 Improve the structure of your work by using:

   a) the 'building blocks' of structure (page 77)

   b) transition words (page 79)

   c) appropriate reasoning strategies (page 80).

3 Examine your work in terms of style

   If you have difficulty in paraphrasing the views of others (such as after research), raising your writing standard above the ordinary, or providing a logical argument, reread section 3.7 (page 83). Use the following questions:

   a) In what way is style evident? (How have the words have been put together?)

b) Are particular attitudes or beliefs evident? (Have you put opposing views?)

c) Is the manner of expression appropriate in terms of the reader and the situation?

d) Do the points follow in logical order?

4 How well have you used evidence?

a) Where recent work is concerned, have you made claims without supporting evidence?

b) Where could you quote more appropriately (or reduce the number of quotes)?

c) Have you clearly distinguished your views from those of others (e.g., by using quotation marks)?

5 Test your summary skills

Select an extended piece of your written work. Using the example on page 92, prepare an abbreviated version. (How does this compare with the original?)

4 Essays

One-minute overview

Study at advanced level requires you to:
- have a thorough knowledge of your subject
- analyse and evaluate evidence
- present compelling arguments, and
- demonstrate competent writing skills.

The essay is a major tool for assessing all these skills. The academic skills and reading required, together with tutor comments, mean that essays have an important developmental function. Properly balanced tutor comments can also play a crucial role in enhancing your self-confidence and creating the desire for further learning.

No matter how experienced you are, the words 'assessed essay' can create apprehension and anxiety. This is all the more reason why essays should be seen as a process consisting of specific skills (such as question analysis and planning) and posing particular challenges (such as establishing and sustaining a convincing argument).

Chapter 4 will help you understand:
- the importance of essays
- what constitutes an effective essay
- common essay problems
- the importance of question analysis
- the planning process
- the elements of structure.

4.1 The importance of essays

Essays are the standard form of assessment at advanced level. But they also have a developmental function, in that they enhance your subject knowledge and improve your thinking and writing skills. Essays also help you with exams in terms of technique and resources.

An essay is, in effect, a logical argument in written form that:

- conveys subject knowledge and understanding

- indicates how this knowledge is interpreted and applied

- demonstrates an evaluation of the relevant ideas, concepts and theories.

So essays help you develop and deepen your knowledge of a subject by involving you in activities such as research, and encouraging you to consider and debate key issues.

Effective essays

In an effective essay you will:

- interpret the question correctly

- highlight the main issues

- indicate wide research

- exhibit a good structure

- demonstrate good writing skills

- provide appropriate evidence

- reach conclusions.

Common problems

Some common problems are:

- misunderstanding the question

- poor introduction

- no logical structure

- contentions without evidence

- straying from the point

- lack of analysis

- poor summary and conclusion.

4.2 Understanding questions

Interpreting and answering the question you have been set
are fundamental essay skills. Answering questions at
advanced level requires not merely the description or
repetition of knowledge itself, but the analysis, evaluation
and interpretation of it. It also entails selecting relevant
information and organising it in a way that directly answers
the question.

Consequently, question analysis is extremely important.
If you do not fully understand the question, you cannot
make a full and appropriate response to it. Your ability to
understand and analyse questions is related to a number of
factors, including:

- previous experience of answering questions

- the quality and appropriateness of research

- knowledge of the subject.

As Figure 4.1 indicates, the process of question analysis
can also be seen as a series of steps such as: identifying the
question type, breaking down the question into its relevant
parts, appreciating the importance and ramifications of the
question, and developing a line of argument (see page 110
for more details)

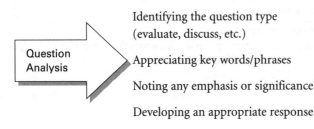

Identifying the question type
(evaluate, discuss, etc.)

Question
Analysis

Appreciating key words/phrases

Noting any emphasis or significance

Developing an appropriate response

*Figure 4.1
Question
analysis*

Types of questions

A comprehensive list of question types is given in Table 4.1, but there are two main approaches:

- the explanation (why) question, e.g., 'How can the ... be explained in the context of ...?')

- the assessment/evaluation question, e.g., 'Discuss and assess ...'.

These two general approaches can be combined to produce:

- the explanation and assessment type, e.g., 'Identify the main ... and assess their importance in relation to ...'.

The question as instruction

All questions contain an instruction. These instructions must be followed exactly, or marks may be deducted for not answering the question.

Table 4.1
Examples of
question types
▼

Account for	*Give reasons for/explain the cause of* Demonstrate your ability and command of the subject by being able to identify and explain matters in response to the question.
Analyse	*Reach an understanding by closely examining the different parts of a topic (breaking things down)* Close examination of the various factors, and perceptive observations are prerequisites for the analytical essay.
Assess	*Make a value judgement about one or more factors* Arrive at an estimation about certain factors or elements, particularly in relation to their effectiveness or consequences
Clarify	*Simplify or make clear* Make certain matters easier to understand through a logical process of explanation.
Comment (on/upon/ critically)	*Give your point of view* Make informed comments about a particular issue, factor or event.

Compare (and contrast)	*Identify similarities and differences* Examine in order to identify similarities and differences between issues, factors or ideas.
Consider	*Think carefully about a particular matter* Consider the merits of a particular topic to produce an answer which is thoughtful and insightful.
Contrast	*Comparison of unlike or opposite qualities* Discuss elements of an issue or topic in order to illustrate their differences.
Criticise	*Judge, analyse or evaluate (with disapproval)* Examine an issue critically, giving evidence to support your opinion.
Define	*State the precise meaning* Test whether a particular (often controversial) term or concept has been understood. Define is usually linked to another instruction, for example, 'briefly define what you mean by the term ... and explain the significance of...' .
Describe	*Give an account of* Great care should be taken with this instruction if it occurs at advanced level, particularly if it is not linked to another instruction. By itself, it merely invites a recitation of facts; if this is the case, carefully consider the whole question.
Discuss	*Examine by argument (debate the pros and cons)* Examine the stated aspects of a subject (often two sides) and weigh their relative merits. This involves presenting evidence, arguments and to a certain extent personal opinion.
Distinguish	*Highlight the differences* This is often used in the first part of a question or instruction to obtain a clearer picture of two or more issues.
Evaluate	*Judge or assess the worth of* This calls for an examination of the merits of a particular issue or case and, consequently, reaching a personal judgement.
Examine	*Scrutinise carefully or in detail; investigate* Conduct a logical, detailed analysis of an issue or case, highlighting elements such as cause and effect.
Explain	*Give a clear and detailed account* Clarify or account for something by selecting details you feel are important.

How	*In what way (to what extent?)* This indicates that there is perhaps no one answer to the question. So key issues have to be identified, arguments made, evidence offered and your final position made clear.
Justify	*Give reasons for/prove* Make out a case for a particular point of view. The use of evidence and strong argument is essential.
Outline	*Give the main features* Select only the essential parts. This is usually followed by a second instruction requiring more detail or an evaluation.
State	*Present briefly and clearly* Give the main features of a topic or case briefly, but clearly.
Summarise	*State the main points* Bring together the main points without going into detail or giving examples.

Table 4.1
Examples of
question types
(contd)

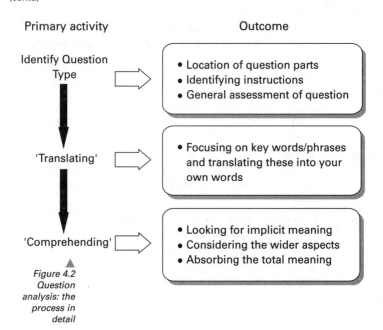

Primary activity   Outcome

Identify Question Type
- Location of question parts
- Identifying instructions
- General assessment of question

'Translating'
- Focusing on key words/phrases and translating these into your own words

'Comprehending'
- Looking for implicit meaning
- Considering the wider aspects
- Absorbing the total meaning

Figure 4.2
Question
analysis: the
process in
detail

Analyse The Question	View question analysis as a process; follow the above example
Assess Your Immediate Response	Consider your immediate response to the question. Do you agree/disagree/partially agree?; offer a different viewpoint?
Give Reasons in Support	List the main points in support of your argument, are they logical/sustainable? (don't forget the opposing argument)
Convert into Paragraphs	Translate the main points into paragraphs and critically appraise (e.g., is there a balanced argument?)
Prepare a Rough Draft	Have you clearly and concisely answered the question set? (have you provided the evidence?)

4.3 Essay planning

Figure 4.3 From question to answer

The essay plan is an overview of what you intend to cover in the essay. Although plans must be flexible enough to allow the inclusion of new ideas or comments, the completed essay should not differ too much from the original plan. Essay planning will also help you perform better in examinations (same process, different timescale).

Focus points: essay planning

Essay planning is essential for:

- organising your thoughts and response to the question
- assessing the strength and effectiveness of your argument
- indicating what research and evidence is required
- providing direction and logical flow
- avoiding digression and waffle

- determining the number, type and content of paragraphs

- testing whether you are answering the question.

An essay plan should start with an analysis and interpretation of the question. You should then be able to adopt a line of argument, develop the argument in a logical, analytical manner and provide some sort of conclusion. There are various approaches to essay planning and the one selected will vary from individual to individual:

- a finely detailed, highly structured, but very effective planned essay

- a series of single words or phrases introducing the key point or idea

- a simple three-stage 'News at Ten' essay.

The 'News at Ten' approach is planned, but the plan is a simple one consisting of:

- Stage 1 – tell them what you are going to say (introduction)

- Stage 2 – say it (main body)

- Stage 3 – tell them what you've said (summary/conclusion).

For example, an essay of 1,000 words may be laid out as follows:

Introduction (100 words or less)	Define key terms and perhaps indicate how you are going to proceed.
Main body (600–700 words)	Deal with the main points, linking them logically.
Summary/conclusion (about 200 words)	Briefly recall the main issues and give a final analysis and assessment.

Planning levels

Whatever type of plan is used, the essay is generally planned at three different levels.

Level 1: As a coherent whole — Each separate paragraph is designed to form one logical, structured and complete statement.

Level 2: Each paragraph is planned — Each sentence is carefully planned to form a clear, concise and sequential paragraph.

Level 3: Each sentence is planned — Precise, pertinent and properly constructed.

The inductive plan (Figure 4.4) appears to be the most popular approach. However, like many aspects of study skills, the best approach is the one that you feel most comfortable with and that works.

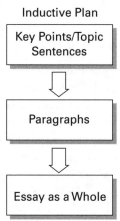

Inductive Plan

Key Points/Topic Sentences

⬇

Paragraphs

⬇

Essay as a Whole

*Figure 4.4
The inductive plan
◄*

The introduction

Many students find that structuring the essay (organising the information) is one of the biggest problems. It is here that the introduction plays an important part. An introduction should consist of no more than two paragraphs and have a good opening sentence.

Focus points: the introduction

An introduction should:

- give a brief interpretation and assessment of the question by:

  - demonstrating that the writer understands key terms

  - indicating how they are going to proceed

- set the scene for the main body

- introduce a line of thought, argument or idea

- act as a link to the first main paragraph.

A good rule of thumb for introductions is that they should be no more than 10% of the overall essay. Indeed, instead of going into detail and spelling out what they are trying to achieve in the essay, some experienced writers use a form of words that implies what they are attempting to achieve. This approach substantially reduces the number of words in the introduction.

The main body

Great skill is required when constructing the various parts of an argument or examining the issues. But if the essay has been planned properly, the main body is often less of a problem than the introduction or conclusion. This does not mean that the main body is less important, but many students find that once they get going it is easy to follow a carefully planned main body because the points or ideas have (or should have) been logically linked.

Focus points: the main body

The main body should contain:

- a detailed account of the argument or issues

- evidence in support of any arguments or contentions

- an evaluation/assessment of the key issues.

The conclusion

The purpose of a conclusion is to re-emphasise particular points made during the course of the essay. Just as the introduction creates an initial impression before the main body is read, the conclusion leaves a lasting impression. In some cases, a good conclusion can help compensate for mistakes in the main body. The conclusion should demonstrate analysis, critical thought and an evaluation of the evidence and the arguments presented.

In most cases, the conclusion will be longer than the introduction, however, some of the most effective conclusions can be no longer than ten lines. This is particularly so, if structure and style (and time) permits the use of a separate summary paragraph before the conclusion

Focus points: the conclusion

A conclusion should contain:

- a brief summary of the key points

- a personal evaluation

- references to the question

- a compelling and impressive statement (if personal style permits).

4.4 Developing essay skills
Sarah's problem

Sarah is studying for a degree in business studies and has just had some of her first essays assessed. Unfortunately, the news is not good. Although Sarah worked hard, she received only pass grades. It was not just the grades that worried her, but the comments as well: lacks structure; straying from the point; much description, little analysis; weak argument; poor conclusion; very one-sided.

Sarah had done well at Higher National Diploma (HND) level and this had encouraged her to progress to a degree. However, she had no real experience of writing essays since her HND course required her only to write reports. After recovering from the initial shock, Sarah went to see her personal tutor. He said that before the next round of assessed essays she must develop her skills. He gave her some general advice and notes on essay writing and recommended that she needed to focus on question analysis, structure, key words and the use of evidence. He also suggested that she should choose a topic that would allow her to develop a clear argument.

Sarah believes that she has such a possible topic. In her recent human resource management (HRM) seminar there was a heated debate about the use of psychometric tests by employers to recruit staff. Her HRM lecturer helped with an essay title and some additional reading. Sarah was now ready to develop an action plan. She decided to:

- analyse the question (page 107)

- list a number of points for and against

- prepare an essay plan (page 111).

Sarah has also decided to adopt a more elaborate essay structure. For example, she has been using the simple structure A (a box represents each paragraph) and now wants to try structure B (see Figure 4.5). As structure A demonstrates, all the points are given for one side of the argument first (normally the points for), a transition (linking) paragraph is written and all the points against are then stated.

The more elaborate structure B involves the construction of an argument in a blow-by-blow fashion. First, the points in support of an argument or theory are outlined (for example, the ones you disagree with), then the opposing points (the ones you agree with) are made in a manner that subtly and effectively undermines the theories, concepts or views you disagree with.

Figure 4.5 Essay structures ▼

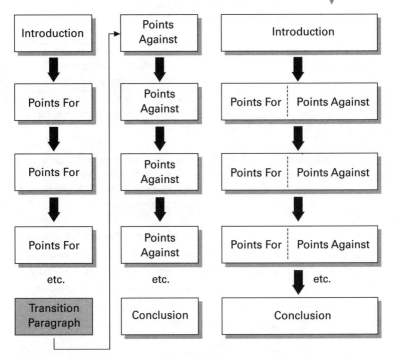

Note. For the purposes of illustration, the 'for' and 'against' paragraphs in structure A are shown side by side. In practice, the 'for' paragraphs might occupy an A4 page or more on their own before the 'against' points are stated. Again, structure B would occupy several pages of A4 depending on the length of the essay.

Figure 4.6 shows the essay question Sarah has selected and her analysis of it. Sarah has also tried to 'translate' the question into her own words.

Figure 4.6 Essay question ▼

"Psychometric tests play an important part in the recruitment and selection process". Discuss

Define

To what extent?

Pros & Cons

Of what value are psychometric tests when recruiting people?

Points for	Points against
Testing has been in use for more than 50 years. However, there has been a significant rise in its use in the last decade	Some have a low validity rate (e.g., personality tests)
Tests are very useful in matching specific job needs	It is crucial that such tests are administered and marked by specialists; many are not
Euro Employment Services report that the use of personality tests has risen by 119% over the past four years	Intelligence is a very complex thing to measure; there is no agreed definition
Tests are very useful in identifying many appropriate or inappropriate jobseekers at once	Even supporters of tests agree that it is wrong to send people home with tests that should be done in a controlled situation

Table 4.2 Points for and against

As well as getting points for and against, Sarah realises that she must get some quotations to use as evidence. Most importantly, she must also produce sentences that explain terms like *psychometric test*. Fortunately, Sarah has found some useful material in a journal for personnel professionals. The following definitions are examples of her notes from the journal:

- Psychometric tests are psychological tests that can be systematically graded.

- These tests are used to measure individual differences; for example, in personality, aptitude, ability, attainment or intelligence.

Table 4.3 Sarah's essay plan ▶

Para 1 (intro)	Define psychometric tests Indicate my approach Mention need to examine validity etc. State what tests are based on Give example of personality tests
Para 2	Evidence of increasing use Use Steve Black quote
Para 3	**Change of direction here** Use another Steve Black quote to counter previous support for tests

Para 4	Use Smith quote to avoid bias Counter Smith quote with Williams to reinforce my line of argument
Para 5	Criticise how tests are actually used Question validity Legal aspects
Para 6	**Linking para** Acknowledge more advantages of tests, but lead into more criticisms
Para 7	Use first, second and third approach to consolidate argument against tests
Para 8	More evidence against tests before summary
Para 9	Briefly recap evidence against tests before mentioning role of manager
Para 10	Conclusion Make it brief Refer back to question Try to turn question on itself

Table 4.3
Sarah's essay plan (contd)
◀

Although Sarah's essay still has to be completed, a one-page overview is shown in the box with key phrases, linking words and references highlighted.

'Psychometric tests play an invaluable part in the recruitment and selection process'. Discuss

1   **Any determination** that psychological tests are an aid to the recruitment and selection process entails an examination of their validity, reliability and the extent and particular circumstances of their use. Such tests are based upon the principle that individual differences with regard to aptitude, ability, intelligence, attainment and personality can be scientifically measured. **For example**, personality tests (pioneered by Raymond Cattell over 44 years ago) are ranged over some 16 behavioural scales and are therefore **held** to be extremely accurate.

2   **Although** testing has been in existence for more than 50 years, there has been a significant rise in its use in

---

the last decade. **Indeed,** Euro Employment Services (EES) reports that the use of personality profiles has risen by 119% over the last four years [1]. **Moreover,** independent survey results indicate that 75% of large organisations now use ability tests; 55% use personality questionnaires tests; and 50% use assessment-centre methods [2]. **The reason for this** is given by Steve Black, Chief Executive of EES, 'Organisations are much more aware that people make the difference...'

3 **Despite this** apparent enthusiasm for psychometric testing, numerous fears have been expressed; some of these misgivings have come from practitioners themselves. Steve Black (ibid) again *comments in this respect*, 'Personality tests are right in just 10–15% of cases. Lots of psychologists are still debating their value, but my own view is that their validity is still very low'.

4 **Conversely,** Ron Smith (2003:17), principal psychologist for a local government organisation, **asserts** that if personality tests are used in a focused way, where the employer is clear about the criteria for job selection, 'they are a useful tool'. **Nevertheless,** Martin Williams (2003:4), an outspoken critic of personality testing **maintains,** 'There is no evidence that personality tests are able to predict job performance...'

5 **More recently,** *evidence has emerged that seriously calls into question* how psychometric tests are actually used. **It was revealed** in 1994 that a number of organisations were using personality tests simply to select people for redundancy (**Morgan, 2003:2**). **Claims with respect to** validity were *also undermined* when it emerged that some companies were allowing tests to be completed at home. **Most seriously,** cases have gone to employment tribunals

where claims were made that psychometric tests discriminated against ethnic minorities (Black, op. cit.).

6 **While** psychometric tests have advantages such as matching certain job traits and needs, identifying many appropriate or inappropriate candidates at one go, and doing so quickly and relatively easily, *substantial criticisms remain.*

7 **First**, while aptitude tests may be *relatively accurate* at one point in time, it is crucial that such tests are administered and scored by trained personnel; yet the evidence regarding misuse of tests *indicates* that this is not always the case. **Second**, not only is intelligence a very complex subject, but it is impossible to categorise all personality traits and other aspects of human behaviour. **Third**, even supporters of psychometric testing point to the very low success rate of personality tests – *yet* these are the very tests that many companies rely upon.

8 **In addition**, it is *generally held* that tests can be rendered invalid by candidates 'second guessing' (trying to determine what the organisation wants and behaving accordingly). **It has also been documented** that psychometric tests can discriminate against minority groups. **Accordingly**, they cannot therefore be as refined and scientific as their supporters suggest.

9 **Further to the substantial evidence against** psychometric testing already examined (poor reliability and validity, their misuse and allegations of their discrimination against minority groups) is the neglected role of the line manager. **It appears somewhat contradictory** that as modern line managers have become more concerned with the people issues of their business, they are most often the individuals who are not allowed to be involved in the process of test interpretation. **Consequently**, the true

> value of psychometric tests will only be realised by organisations that are able to bridge the gap between tests scores and meaningful management action.
>
> 10 **Thus,** the fact that psychometric tests are held to be an invaluable aid to the selection process is, in itself, a value judgement and a self-fulfilling prophecy.

Tutor's comments

Paragraph 1 Although this is a relatively short introduction, it fulfils most of the requirements: it refers to the question; it introduces a line of thought; it indicates how Sarah is going to proceed; and it provides a link to the first main paragraph. Importantly, the words, 'any determination' also reveal that Sarah does not agree with the position indicated in the question, i.e., that psychometric tests are an invaluable aid to the recruitment process. Also, Sarah explains the principles behind psychometric testing and cannot ignore the many years they have been in use. However, by using the word *held* Sarah again reveals her opposition to the claim implied in the essay title and subtly undermines the objective information provided in this paragraph.

Paragraph 2 Aware of previous tutor comments about bias, Sarah realises that she must continue to provide more objective information about the tests (she can use the more elaborate 'for and against' paragraph structure to counteract this later). Key words such as *although*, *indeed* and *moreover*, along with the quotation, help consolidate this good developing paragraph.

Paragraph 3 The use of the words, 'Despite this' indicates that this is an important transition paragraph which changes the direction of the essay. By using terms such as 'numerous fears' and 'misgivings', coupled with the critical quote regarding personality tests, Sarah has undermined the information provided in paragraph three (supporting the use of tests). This is an excellent example of effective essay technique.

Paragraph 4 Again, to avoid bias, Sarah introduces some more evidence to support the use of personality tests. However, she is careful to finish with a quote that supports her position. This paragraph could have been part of the preceding one. But by choosing to make it a separate paragraph Sarah creates another opportunity to avoid the appearance of bias and, at the same time, introduce more evidence to support her argument.

Paragraph 5 This paragraph leaves no doubt about Sarah's approach to the question. Using a sequence of evidence technique (such as 'More recently', 'It was revealed' and 'Most seriously'), she starts to launch a major argument against the claim that psychometric tests play an important part in the recruitment and selection process.

Paragraph 6 Before continuing her effective indictment of testing in the next paragraph, Sarah pauses her attack briefly to state some of the main advantages of testing. The use of the term 'substantial criticisms remain' signals that not only is this an important linking paragraph, but also that there are more critical points to follow.

Paragraph 7 In this paragraph Sarah really demonstrates her command of the blow-by-blow paragraph technique. She is careful to select only three but crucial key points concerning tests (accuracy, the complex nature of intelligence and the low success rate of personality tests) and criticise these one by one. Sarah is also careful to stop at 'third'. To continue this listing technique ('fourth', 'fifth' and so on) would have undermined the impact of this very effective paragraph.

Paragraph 8 By creating this new but linked paragraph, Sarah has maximised the impact of the previous one. By using the words, 'in addition' the reader is left in no doubt that more related points are to be made. This is the last paragraph before the summary of key points in the next.

Paragraph 9 Not only is this a summary paragraph as indicated, but Sarah has taken the risk at this late point in the essay to introduce a new point: the role of the manager (in doing so, she also reaches a conclusion). This is risky because it could upset the balance of the essay and lead Sarah off the point. Skilfully done, however, this can be a powerful technique since it demonstrates that the writer is not only answering the question set, but also considering the wider ramifications and/or raising the debate to a higher level.

Paragraph 10 Like some others, this paragraph could have been joined with the previous one to form a complete whole. In this case, there would have been one final paragraph with no separate summary. Once again, by choosing to form a separate paragraph, Sarah has drawn greater attention to the points made in the previous one. This short final paragraph is quite powerful since it also accomplishes three main things: first, like all final paragraphs should, it refers back to the question; second, it attacks the question itself for implying a value judgement; third, it finally reinforces Sarah's main argument.

In Sarah's more complete final version, her sources will be documented during the essay (for example, Morgan, 2003:2) and at the end in a bibliography (review pages 99–100).

General comments

Although this is only a one-page overview of Sarah's essay, it is a vast improvement on her previous attempts. She has used the more elaborate paragraph technique with skill and wide reading is apparent. Evidence is used very effectively.

The overview indicates that the finished essay will be very good, demonstrating fluency and a command of the key techniques of essay writing, particularly the ability to develop an argument. The essay that Sarah will produce is proof that negative tutor comments, if acted upon, do not necessarily mean that all is lost.

Focus points: Sarah's essay

- Do not be disappointed if you get negative essay feedback – turn it to your advantage.

- Seek and act upon tutors' advice.

- Read the question carefully and practise question analysis (page 107).

- Choose a structure you feel comfortable with (page 112).

- Research as widely as time permits (lecture notes alone are not enough).

- Develop a list of key points ('for' or 'against' if appropriate – see page 112).

- Create an essay plan (pages 111, 112 and 113).

- Plan where and when to use evidence (don't forget to document sources).

- If possible, plan impressive opening and closing phrases.

- Write a rough draft.

Summary

- An essay is a logical argument in writing which conveys subject knowledge and understanding, and indicates how this is interpreted, applied and evaluated.

- An effective essay interprets the question correctly, highlights the main issues, indicates wide research and has a good structure. It also demonstrates good writing skills, contains appropriate evidence and reaches conclusions.

- Identifying the question type and the instruction it contains is crucial to answering the question set.

- An essay plan should start with an analysis and interpretation of the question. This will enable you to adopt a line of argument, continue this logically and analytically, and provide some sort of conclusion.

- Whatever type of plan is used, an essay is essentially planned at three levels: the essay as a whole, the main paragraphs and the key sentences.

Tutorial

1 If you wish to develop your essay skills before starting a course, or before producing assessed essays, write a list of controversial topics and follow Sarah's approach. Here are some suggestions to help you:

- blood sports

- nuclear power

- social welfare

- euthanasia

- equal opportunities

- the role of women

- politics in general

- education

- the environment

- law and order issues

2 Evaluate some of your recent essays using this chapter as a general checklist. Although you may have already identified areas for improvement, look particularly at structure, the use of evidence and

writing skill. Could you have improved your efforts? (How?)

3 When you are given the next formal or assessed essay:

a) identify the question type

b) follow the process of question analysis

c) identify the main points

d) develop a suitable essay plan and structure

e) write a rough draft and critically review.

Note. Don't forget to review and use Chapter 3 on writing skills.

5

Reports and dissertations

Reports

It is becoming increasingly necessary for students on certain types of academic courses to be able to write clear, concise and effective reports. This is also an important business skill. Report writing differs from essay writing in several ways, particularly with regard to writing style, the emphasis on factual information (actual events) and the method of presentation (format). Although students may not always be dealing with actual events, they will have to conform to style and format.

This chapter will:

- discuss how reports arise in different contexts and at different points in time
- explain the different aspects of short informal and short formal reports
- advise on the various stages of report writing
- provide a report-writing checklist.

Dissertations

Dissertations are an important part of assessment on the majority of courses at degree level. The success of your dissertation depends on a number of factors, including the selection of a topic (see page 143), developing a proposal, the generation of relevant and quality information or data, analysing the information, providing a suitable framework, and anticipating and overcoming problems.

This chapter will:

- explain the importance of a proposal
- provide a suitable dissertation framework
- identify how relevant information can be generated (organisations)
- raise awareness about potential problems.

5.1 Reports

The term *report* is used to describe a variety of written material from memoranda to dissertations. Reports can take a number of forms and differ in length, scope and presentation. They range from simple memoranda to technical, scientific and more extensive reports associated with large companies and government organisations.

Here the term is used in the context of a business report, that is, to examine or investigate an issue or problem, communicate the findings, reach conclusions, and if required, make recommendations.

Figure 5.1
Different
contexts and
points in time
▶

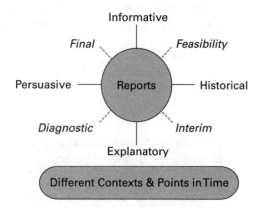

Reports are written for a variety of reasons:

- presenting facts and information (informative)

- recording an event or events (historical)

- answering questions/explaining (explanatory)

- seeking to influence (persuasive).

In a sense, many reports are historical since they are written after the event(s). The nature of the particular report will largely determine which of the above elements is present, or which will have specific influence. It is possible for a report to contain all of them. For example, an accident report in an organisation could:

- contain an account of the *historical* nature of a working practice

- give general *information* related to the accident

- offer an *explanation* of specific events surrounding the accident, –

- *persuade* workers to adopt safer working practices.

There can also be a sequential element to report writing. For example, a company wishing to start a new business venture might commission a feasibility report to determine whether the project is viable. If it decided to proceed, an interim report might be requested to assess issues such as progress and costs. Few projects are problem-free, and a diagnostic report might be necessary. When the project is complete, a final report might be written to examine a range of issues, particularly what lessons can be learned. These two examples (accident reports and the business venture) illustrate the fact that reports arise in different contexts and at different points in time.

5.2 Report writing and students

Depending upon the type of course, students can have various experiences of report writing. For example, engineering students may have to write a technical report; science students may write up the results of an experiment in report form; business or administration studies students may be required to write reports in a business format.

Report writing can be confusing for students in certain circumstances. Figure 5.2 illustrates Brian's academic progress. In each of his courses he had to adapt to a different form of assessment. He developed his essay skills to complete his 'A' levels successfully. Then he took a Higher National Diploma (HND) that required him to write reports. After obtaining his HND, Brian decided to take a degree. Although study at undergraduate level is largely assessed by essays, Brian's course in business studies also required him to write reports and tackle case studies. So not only was Brian changing between different written formats, which involved different styles of expression, he was also required to learn different ways of thinking and problem-solving. Although this is excellent training, it can be confusing at times.

Figure 5.2
Different forms
of assessment
▶

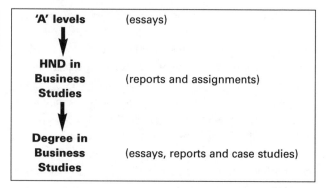

'A' levels   (essays)

HND in
Business   (reports and assignments)
Studies

Degree in
Business   (essays, reports and case studies)
Studies

5.3 Types of report

Students are normally asked to write two main types of report: short formal reports and short informal reports. Although informal reports can have numbered headings and subheadings as used in formal reports (see page 136), it is better to use simple headings unless requested to do otherwise.

The short informal report

As its name implies, the short informal report has a simple structure which usually consists of three stages:

Stage 1: Introduction   The opening stage provides the background information, puts the report into context and outlines the situation

Stage 2: Problem/issue examined	The middle stage reveals the relevant information that has been collected and analysed (the findings)
Stage 3: Conclusion	The final stage summarises the main points, makes conclusions and, if required, gives recommendations

The short formal report

As can be seen from the components in Figure 5.3, the short formal report has a more elaborate structure than the short informal report. Although you may not be required to provide a summary, it is important to remember that a summary (sometimes known in business reports as an *executive synopsis*) is an essential part of many formal reports. Consequently, the layout of the short formal report on page 137 contains both a summary and a contents page as well as the basic components illustrated in Figure 5.3.

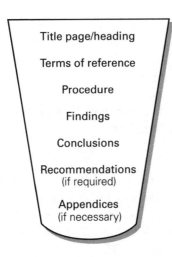

Title page/heading

Terms of reference

Procedure

Findings

Conclusions

Recommendations
(if required)

Appendices
(if necessary)

Figure 5.3
The short
formal report:
basic
components
◄

The differences between short informal and short formal reports are listed in Table 5.1.

Short informal report	Short formal report
A few sides of A4	Can be extensive (3000–4000 words)
Basic three-stage approach	More elaborate structure
No title page required	Title page often used
A simple introduction	Terms of reference section and details of the investigation procedure used (if relevant)
Simple system of headings	Formal (decimal) referencing system
Usually no summary	Summary provided
Informal language (but good grammar)	More formal tone (third person)

Example of a short informal report (extract)

Confidential

For: The Principal   Ref: JS/P30

From: John Smith, Director of
        Student Services   Date: May 14th 2004

Report on Student Services (non-academic)

INTRODUCTION

On Friday May 2nd, you asked me to investigate the current state of student facilities, and to make recommendations where appropriate. In addition to my own investigations, the report also includes informal feedback from elected student representatives. The student counselling service and the accommodations unit are excluded from this report, which was to be submitted to you no later than May 16th.

FINDINGS

General accommodation

For the purposes of association, students only have one room in the main building (A11), and none in either of the two annexes. They have access, of course, to the main gymnasium and the new polygym (C block), but must compete with staff and some sixth formers from St George's School.

Refectory services

On the main site, students are served by the large refectory in A block which dispenses hot meals at peak hours; the small eating area in D block is serviced solely by vending machines. A soft drinks machine is the only refreshment facility in each of the annexes.

Quality of facilities

The 'students room' in the main building contains a snooker table, bench-type seating and a soft drinks machine; an old radio provides background music. This room also doubles as a venue for the various student clubs and interest groups; there is no access for disabled students. Students appreciate the new polygym, but limited access to its facilities limits its impact. The main gymnasium is under-utilised through lack of facilities. However, badminton, table tennis and even squash would be possible with minor alterations and the purchase of additional equipment.

Although the refectory staff do their best under the current financial constraints, the service provided is best described as adequate. Many students have commented that the menu is rather limited, with the emphasis on fast food. A substantial number of students have also complained that there is no smoke-free zone within the refectory areas.

CONCLUSION AND RECOMMENDATIONS

The investigations made, along with the comments of elected student representatives, indicate that immediate, comprehensive steps need to be taken to improve student facilities. The following therefore, are recommended for your consideration:

a) For the purposes of association, the provision of one additional room in the main building, and one room in each of the two annexes (suitably furnished).

b) One of the two rooms in the main building, and part of each of the new rooms in the annexes should be designated as no smoking areas.

c) The existing 'students room' in the main building should be refurbished, with casual seating and a television and juke box provided.

Note. The headings 'introduction' 'findings' and 'conclusions and recommendations' are for illustrative purposes and need not appear in the actual report.

Example of a short formal report (extract)

Confidential

For: The Principal   Ref: RS/P/HS9

From: Ron Scott, College Safety
        Officer   Date: March 18th 2004

Report on Current Health and Safety Standards

1.0 Summary

1.1 Accidents occurred to nine people and were minor in nature. They fell into the following categories: unsafe working practices/careless behaviour, equipment failure and miscellaneous matters.

Key Questions	Answered in	Example of Contents

What is the report about?	**Title Page**	• Should indicate clearly and concisely
		   – What the report is about
		   – Who will receive it
		   – Date, circulation and reference number
		   – Classification, e.g., confidential.

How is the report divided?	**Contents Page**	• Reference to section headings • Page numbers (and paragraph numbers if long report)
What are the main findings?	**Summary**	• Comments on the key areas
What has the writer been asked to do?	**Terms of Reference** (introduction)	• Main areas of investigation/ analysis • Any constraints and problems
How was the information gained?	**Procedure**	• Interviews?, Observation?, Reading?, Experiments?
The main findings in detail? *What picture emerges?*	**Body of the Report Conclusions**	• Presentation of the facts in full • Must be related to the facts outlined in the body of the report
What actions are required?	**Recommendations**	• Must state clearly which solutions/option is the most effective (and why)
Where is the evidence?	**Appendices**	• Contains supporting evidence such as diagrams, financial & technical data • Items are placed here so that the flow of the report is not interrupted

Figure 5.4 The short formal report: components and structure

1.2 A survey of college premises confirmed that the college is discharging its obligations with regard to health and safety regulations, but a number of concerns were revealed.

1.2.1 The blocking of corridors and stairways

1.2.2 The discarding of lighted cigarettes

1.2.3 Lack of knowledge on the part of teaching staff with regard to first-aiders and specific assembly points

1.2.4 Some students fail to use the safety equipment provided

2.0 Terms of reference

As requested by you at our meeting on March 1st, I have carried out a thorough investigation of health and safety within the main college site and the two annexes. As you also requested, I have made recommendations where appropriate.

3.0 Procedure

3.1 A detailed survey of the main college site and both annexes was conducted with the help of departmental safety representatives.

3.2 All reported accidents during the last college year (and those occurring to date) have been analysed.

3.3 Meetings have been held with departmental safety representatives, trade union representatives, department heads, fire service personnel, and the Health and Safety Inspectorate.

4.0 Findings

4.1 Two students (from engineering and construction respectively) were treated by the college nurse for injuries caused by not using or wearing the safety equipment provided etc.

5.0 Conclusions

5.1 In spite of the many potential hazardous practices that staff and students have to engage in as part of their work, the number of accidents during the period in question was quite small. However, those responsible for safety are not complacent. In general, the college is making every effort to discharge its responsibility with respect to health and safety matters; this fact was commented upon by the parties mentioned in 3.3. Nevertheless, in order to raise the existing high standard of health and safety even further, a number of measures are recommended.

6.0 Recommendations

6.1 An immediate reinforcement of the ban on students blocking stairways.

6.2 College cleaners to stop using the cheaper but more slippery floor cleaner.

6.3 An immediate check on all chairs, particularly the metal frame type.

6.4 Safety rails to be installed on all ramps for the disabled.

6.5 A separate review to be carried out regarding the storage of highly dangerous materials on all college sites.

Ron Scott

College Safety Officer

5.4 Other aspects of reports
Language

Formal reports should be written in the third person (see page 88) to convey objectivity and a professional approach. This style also helps to avoid the tedious repetition of personal pronouns such as 'I' and 'we'. Another advantage of this approach is that it places the emphasis on the subject of the report rather than the writer. For example:

• 'I found out' (first person)

• 'Research revealed' (third person)

Referencing systems

A number of different referencing systems can be used, and all are equally valid. The system of numbered paragraphs and sub-paragraphs illustrated on pages 136–139 is simple to use and is the most appropriate one for students' formal reports. It is important to note that sub-points are indented (moved in from the left-hand side), and further sub-points are indented again. Since extensive points may have to be made, it is equally important to ensure that both main points and sub-points run sequentially and are properly numbered.

Top tip
● Leave sub-point referencing until final editing has been completed.

Conclusions and recommendations

In a business report, you may be asked just to provide findings, and the conclusions and recommendations will be made by others. However, since these two elements indicate analytical skill, students are invariably required to include them. Usually, recommendations come at the end of a report. But if a report is long, it may be more useful to place individual recommendations at the end of the relevant section (this does not prevent a full list of recommendations being placed at the end of the report).

Report writing stages: POWER

Preparing – check the accuracy of information

– consider the aims and objectives of the report

– select the format (informal or formal?)

– consider the reader, plan the report logically

Organising – decide on the main sections/headings

– choose a title that is clear and self-explanatory

– is there going to be a summary and/or an appendix?

– if it is a long report, locate recommendations sensibly

Writing
– use a business-like objective tone

– be clear, concise and factual

– if possible, keep sentences short

– the style should be appropriate to the reader, subject and situation

Editing and
– check the information (could any items be misinterpreted?)

Revising
– examine the contents (do they relate appropriately to the aims, objectives, title and terms of reference?)

– scrutinise for flow (do the findings, conclusions recommendations etc. follow each other sensibly?)

– final check for referencing system/headings, grammar, spelling, appendices etc.

Report writing rules

A report should be:

● **Relevant:** everything in the report should be related to the introduction, terms of reference or the particular situation

● **Appropriate:** all aspects of the report (length, vocabulary, sentence structure, etc.) should be appropriate to the reader and the situation

● **Objective:** all comments must be based solely on the facts and devoid of any personal remarks (except where recommendations are called for)

- **Thorough:** all aspects of the particular problem or issue must be referred to

- **Organised:** sections should be clear, concise, logical, sequential and appropriately referenced

Checklist: report writing

- Be clear about your remit and any constraints. (Introduction/terms of reference.)

- Decide on the main issues/areas of investigation. (Report sections.)

- How is the information to be gathered? (Procedure.)

- What kind of information/data resulted? (Main findings.)

- What kind of format? (Formal or informal?)

- Are the sections logical and sequential? (Flow.)

- Is a summary required? (Report format or length.)

- What are the conclusions? (Analysis.)

- What are the recommendations? (Action required.)

- Are the terminology and tone correct? (Reader, format and context.)

5.5 Dissertations

The term *dissertation* is used in the context of a written piece of research at degree level. Since many of the issues relating to special projects such as dissertations have already been covered (see pages 38–54), this section will provide a framework, consider some common mistakes and offer general advice.

The mistakes associated with dissertations are similar to those associated with other written formats. But because dissertations represent study at degree level they are often considered more seriously. Subject to the differences between the preferred house style of individual universities and colleges, the framework illustrated in Figure 5.5 is generally acceptable.

5.6 The dissertation topic

Figure 5.5
Dissertation framework

The selection of a topic for special projects was discussed on pages 42–44 and most of this information is relevant to dissertations. However, it is not easy to choose a topic that will have to be developed to around 10,000 words (the length of the average dissertation at undergraduate level) and bear detailed examination. Therefore, it is not unusual for students to select a topic either in haste (because of limited interest) or simply because they have access to particular information.

Although it is useful if the dissertation topic has current relevance or value in itself, several aspects are crucial to success:

- The writer/researcher must have a genuine interest in the area chosen for investigation.

- All the necessary information must be available.

- The topic chosen must lend itself to investigation and analysis at degree level.

Note. Not all the areas of a topic may lend themselves to analysis, so it is important to prioritise the areas that do. Failure to do so can reduce sections of the dissertation to mere description.

Title page

Acknowledgements

Preface/Introduction
(summary)

List of Contents
– main contents
– list of figures
– list of abbreviations
– list of appendices

Abstract

Literature Review

Methodology

Main Chapters/Sections
(plus interim/final conclusions)

Appendices

Bibliography

References

5.7 Generating information

As well as using the methods for generating information outlined in Chapter 2, researchers may wish to get help from a company or organisation, or, indeed, base their research on an organisational problem. Generating information in such a context can involve a number of problems:

- the researcher underestimates the considerable time needed

- issues of confidentiality can arise (e.g., financial data)

- the organisation may have difficulty in allocating the time and other resources necessary for the proposed research.

Consideration of such problems is an important factor in deciding whether or not the proposed research is a viable proposition. Problems can be minimised or avoided by using a range of strategies. For example:

- **Do your homework:** be clear about the aims, objectives and the information required (how will the information relate to the hypothesis or the problems identified?).

- **Be organised:** develop an effective research plan and research log (review pages 44–53).

- **Start early:** contact the organisation as early as possible with full details of the research and information required. If possible, indicate how the research might benefit them.

- **Identify key personnel:** identify a contact person in the organisation and build a rapport as quickly as possible.

- **Identify with their problems:** meet issues such as confidentiality head on. This will help assure them that you take these issues seriously, and appreciate their position.

- **Meet their anxieties:** be prepared to let them see your work periodically (inform them of this at the earliest opportunity).

- **Think laterally:** identify alternative sources for sensitive information. Innovative solutions or recommendations may also be required (review pages 45–53).

Focus points: potential problems

Although a dissertation framework makes the presentation of information/data more manageable, it does not guarantee logic, analysis, linkage of ideas and overall structure. It is not unusual, therefore, for dissertations to be submitted which:

- have an inadequate introduction (or none at all)

- present a collection of facts with little logic, interpretation or analysis

- contain information that is not relevant to the hypothesis or the aims and objectives

- have a poor general layout/format

- use headings inconsistently

- have an unacceptable level of misspellings or typographical errors

- have abbreviations which are inconsistent, incomplete or absent

- demonstrate poor writing skills in general

- have no conclusions or solutions to the problem(s) identified

- have insufficient detail regarding the actual research methods, such as the number of questionnaires or the sampling techniques used.

5.8 The proposal

Students are normally required to submit a research proposal before starting a dissertation. A proposal is a short outline of the intended dissertation covering areas as the choice of topic, aims and objectives, research methods and so on. It is an important aspect of planning. Your proposal will enable you and your tutor or supervisor to assess how viable the project is, clarify associated issues and identify potential problems. It must answer the key questions referred to in page 40 and have a working title.

Focus points: the proposal

You should:

- clearly indicate the overall approach you are going to take

- confirm (don't assume) that all the relevant information is available

- identify the research methods to be used

- clarify aims and objectives

- provide a realistic work schedule.

Checklist: dissertation

- Choose the area of research carefully.

- Prepare a detailed proposal.

- Keep in regular contact with your tutor or supervisor and inform them of any changes or problems.

- Start researching early – work to a research plan and detailed schedule (effective time management is crucial).

- Choose a suitable framework which helps you to link ideas and conforms to the recommendations of your college or university.

- If your research involves an organisation, pay particular attention to the recommendations outlined in section 5.7.

- Write up work as you go along, rather than generate a mass of notes.

- Check your work periodically for errors, especially in the areas of structure, methodology and presentation.

Summary
Reports

- Students are normally required to write two main types of report: short informal and short formal.

- The short informal report has a simple three-stage structure with simple headings. The short formal report has a more elaborate format which includes a terms of reference section, a formal referencing system and, if required, appendices.

- Important areas include language, referencing and conclusions.

- It is useful to see reports in stages, such as preparing, organising, writing and revising.

- The rules of good report writing include relevance, appropriateness, objectivity, thoroughness and organisation.

Dissertations

- A dissertation is an extensive written piece of research at degree level.

- A dissertation topic must not be selected hastily, because of limited interest, or simply because certain information is available.

- Dissertations must conform to an acceptable format (layout).

- The proposal is an important aspect of planning.

- If a dissertation requires the help of organisations, there may be problems such as underestimating the time necessary to generate the information, issues of confidentiality, and the extent to which organisations can commit time and other resources.

● Dissertations are often flawed by lack of planning in respect of structure, methodology and presentation.

Tutorial

1 Using an informal format and assuming the role of a tutor, write a report about your academic progress to date. What problems does this exercise highlight in terms of objectivity, language and tone?

2 If you are studying at the level which requires a dissertation, and this involves seeking the help of an organisation, draw up a research plan which identifies:

a) your aims and objectives

b) details of the information required

c) how you are going to get the information (your research methodology)

d) a list of key questions

e) how the information will be analysed (and how such information relates to the aims and objectives)

f) a realistic research schedule.

6

Case studies

Case studies are increasingly being used to develop and assess a variety of skills across a range of courses. One of the reasons for this is the belief that, in certain situations, they are a more realistic way of developing and testing an individual's potential to evaluate information, solve problems and make decisions.

Case studies can be presented in different forms, such as in writing, verbally or as role-plays.

This chapter will:

- discuss the importance of case studies as a learning method
- outline the main stages in dealing with case studies
- indicate the different methods of problem-solving which can be used in case studies
- illustrate the different types of knowledge and associated skills which can be developed and assessed by using case studies.

6.1 The nature of case studies

Case studies are now used across a wide range of courses and in a variety of teaching and assessment settings. Some professional bodies are including case studies in their examinations because they provide evidence of the ability to apply skills in a wider, more realistic context, rather than simply answering questions in a repetitive, theoretical way.

Focus points: case studies

As well as linking theory with real-life situations, case studies help you develop the ability to:

- analyse complex situations and apply critical thinking skills

- think creatively and innovatively as well as logically

- view matters objectively and perceive the wider aspects of a situation

- identify problems and generate a range of alternative solutions

- set priorities

- make and evaluate decisions

- view issues in different timescales (short-term and long-term implications)

- handle a variety of information

- communicate effectively with others (joint case analysis).

Case studies can be based on a range of issues presented to students in different formats and approached in a variety of ways. For example, case studies in business and management may involve general organisational and management issues, personnel matters, health and safety, finance and marketing.

Presentation formats include written information, verbal information, in-tray exercises (students are given items such as memos, letters and reports that represent the contents of someone's in-tray at work), role-plays, video or film.

The way in which case studies are approached is crucial, and the particular method depends upon what skills are being developed and what part of the syllabus the tutor is trying to assess. For instance, the case study may take the form of an individual assignment (to be presented verbally or in the form of a report), a group project or a discussion. When case studies are used in examinations, they can be 'seen' or 'unseen'. That is, the student is given the case study to read some time before the exam (seen), but will not have prior knowledge of the questions or tasks; or the student is given the case study on the day of the examination ('unseen').

6.2 Dealing with case studies

Whatever the case study type, it is important to approach it in key stages (see Figure 6.1).

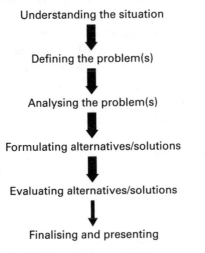

Understanding the situation

Defining the problem(s)

Analysing the problem(s)

Formulating alternatives/solutions

Evaluating alternatives/solutions

Finalising and presenting

*Figure 6.1
Case study
stages*

Understanding the situation

This entails reviewing the material several times to gain a better understanding and to organise the information. At this initial stage it is important to separate fact from opinion, determine what issues are implied as well as stated, and identify what assumptions can be made. Business and management case studies can be examined in terms of such things as processes, people, strategies, objectives (short-term and long-term), resources, organisational structures, management issues, work roles, organisational change and different types of problems.

Defining the problem

It is advisable to clarify the key issues, identify which items of information are relevant, and separate cause from effect.

Problems can be apparent or hidden, occur in the present or future and can have short-term or long-term implications. Problem identification involves making assumptions, drawing conclusions, taking values into account and assessing the various factors. Defining problems also means not jumping to conclusions too quickly.

It is sometimes possible to distinguish between 'closed' and 'open' problems. Closed problems generally indicate answers that are the logical outcome of the stated or known facts. In open problems the stated or known facts may be imprecise, not clearly defined or in dispute. In terms of approaches to problem-solving, the analytical approach is often associated with closed problems and more creative approaches are linked to open problems.

A simple but effective way of identifying problems in general, but particularly where case studies are concerned, is the 5WH approach. An illustration of how this method can be used to ask key questions relating to case studies appears in the box.

What	are the main issues? are the main objectives? constraints are there? are the key problems? decisions need to be made?	**Why**	is the problem occurring? is it a problem? is analysis difficult? are certain items/factors necessary? are some solutions inappropriate?
Where	is the key information? are values apparent? do needs conflict? do priorities need to be made? do changes need to be made? are solutions implied?	**Who**	are the key players in the situation? causes/contributes to the problem? is affected by the problem? can help with the problem? will be affected by the decisions?
When	does the problem(s) occur? do certain factors come into play?	**How**	big is the problem? does it affect other issues? is it done (procedures, etc.)?

When (contd)	can judgements be made? are alternatives possible? do decisions have to be made (timescale)?	How (contd)	else could it be done? will decisions be evaluated? will decisions be implemented?

Analysing the problem

Analysing anything implicitly involves:

- different approaches to thinking

- the skills of thinking

- viewing problem-solving as a process.

Problem-solving by thinking is often seen as consisting of two main approaches: analytical (logical) thinking and creative (lateral) thinking. Figure 6.2 shows the main components of these two approaches.

Figure 6.2 Analytical and creative thinking

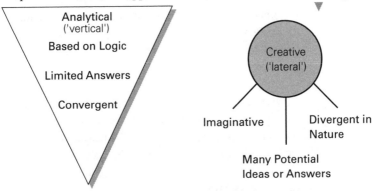

A widely held view is that conventional approaches to problem-solving such as *logical progression* (moving from one step to another – from step 1 to step 2 and so on) prevent you reaching satisfactory solutions, particularly if the potential solution is an innovative one. For example, it is suggested that where problem analysis is concerned, instead of thinking (conventionally) 'what is the problem', you should be thinking (creatively) 'what is not the problem'. This example of a novel approach allows you to unload 'unwanted baggage', permitting you to eliminate immediately those elements that are not really relevant to the solution.

Unlike logical (convergent) thinking, creative thinking is wide-ranging and requires intuition, imagination, the desire to challenge the obvious and the ability to relate factors which were previously unrelated. For example, a farmer faced with the problem that his existing machinery cannot cope with harvesting the increasingly irregular branches of his apple trees might ask engineers to design a new machine (logical thinking). Or he could ask plant scientists to 'design' a new tree where the branches grow to a certain height and overall circumference (lateral thinking).

An important feature of creative thinking is brainstorming. Because brainstorming is such a creative process, there is a tendency to see it as lacking in structure. Not only are there rules to brainstorming (such as define the problem and discuss, redefine the problem and discuss), but logical processes are used to evaluate the ideas or solutions generated by the brainstorming technique.

Originally, brainstorming was applied to group activities where a large number of ideas were generated in a short time. However, it is possible for individuals to use a similar technique by adopting the features indicated below.

Focus points: brainstorming

- Restate or reformulate the problem.

- Think laterally.

- Generate as many ideas as possible.

- Consider 'far out' or unlikely ideas.

- Change emphasis from one part of the problem to another.

- All ideas are acceptable until proved otherwise (suspend immediate judgement).

Barriers to problem-solving

There are several barriers to solving problems effectively:

One right answer. Previous experience (perhaps your school years) leads you to believe that there must be one correct answer. The reality is that some solutions may be more suitable than others, but it is unusual for there to be one perfect answer (otherwise perhaps, it wouldn't be a problem in the first place).

Solution. Use brainstorming techniques.

Accepting ideas too readily. Although the situation in education has changed dramatically, and individuals are now encouraged to challenge conventional and accepted 'truths' (in certain respects), other social experiences influence you to conform. This can have a negative effect on your thinking processes, causing you to accept some things as facts without question.

Solution. Use the 5WH approach – question everything.

Being over-logical. Again, previous experience may lead you to approach every problem in a logical, step-by-step manner. Every problem almost becomes a self-fulfilling prophecy (the desire for one logical solution clouds your ability to arrive at innovative solutions which may be better).

Solution. By all means be logical, but not exclusively so. Don't be afraid to: think laterally, be open-minded, intuitive and imaginative. Also, try jumping (moving illogically) between the various parts of the problem.

Problem-solving skills

There are a variety of skills associated with problem-solving:

Perception	Appreciating that there is/might be a problem in the first place, and identifying its various facets

The ability to perceive potential alternatives/solutions

Being able to visualise the situation that might exist if the problem was solved

Analysis	Breaking down the problem into its various parts
Synthesis	Putting the various parts back together to reconsider the nature of the problem and how these parts may affect each other
Creativity	The ability to think creatively and imaginatively
Evaluation	Evaluating facts and information
	Evaluating any explicit or implied values
	Evaluating potential alternatives /solutions

Focus points: improving problem-solving skills

You can improve your problem-solving skills by adopting different approaches. For example:

- view problem-solving as process

- use a problem-solving model (such as the 5WH strategy)

- use more creative strategies (such as lateral thinking)

- use others as a resource (e.g., brainstorming)

- practise forward thinking (anticipating the solved situation).

Checklist: formulating and evaluating alternatives

Much of what has been said in connection with creative thinking is directly related to formulating alternatives and solutions in relation to case studies. However, various steps can be seen to be crucial:

- establishing a search strategy for generating new and relevant information

- assessing the impact of this information on that already held

- considering the ways in which such information can lead to viable alternatives/solutions

- identifying feasible alternatives/solutions.

Key questions: evaluating alternatives

Evaluating alternatives or solutions is the consolidation stage in determining what alternatives or solutions are suitable for a particular case study. At the evaluation stage, key questions need to be asked:

- What are the consequences of alternative or solution a, b, c?

- How successful is a, b, c likely to be?

- What would happen if a, b or c was selected, existed or applied?

6.3 Finalising and presenting

Finalising involves thoroughly checking that each aspect of the case study is relevant to the tasks set, especially those concerning the decisions taken, the reasons (justification) for those decisions and the recommendations for their implementation. Whether or not the case study guidelines specifically ask for an action plan, it is always good practice to provide one.

Most case study guidelines stipulate how the results are to be presented, and you should follow these closely. Increasingly, students are asked to present their findings and recommendations verbally. The skills required for verbal presentations are discussed in Chapter 7. It is important to master these skills if this method of presentation plays a significant part in the grade awarded.

Review Material

– Organise The Information
– Understand The Situation
– Identify The Key Issues

Prepare For Presentation

– Check Each Aspect
– Review Decisions Taken
– Devise Action Plan
– Choose Method Of Presentation

Clarify Key Issues

– Identify Relevant Information
– Separate Cause From Effect
– Define Problem

Formulate Alternatives

– Identify Possible Alternative
– Consider Values, Priorities etc.
– Evaluate The Consequences

Analyse Problem

– Apply Logic
– Be Creative
– Use a Problem-solving Model
– Consider The Short & Long-term

Figure 6.3
Dealing with
case studies

Checklist: case studies

● Read the case study.

● Organise the information.

● Use aids such as pattern diagrams to help analysis.

● Identify the key issues.

● Use different problem-solving strategies.

● View the issues from different perspectives.

● Identify cause and effect.

● Don't make premature judgements.

● Consider short-term and long-term implications.

- Apply the SWOT concept to the case in general (that is, consider the Strengths, Weaknesses, Opportunities and Threats).

Summary

- Some of the advantages of case studies compared with other learning methods are that they help students to link theory with real-life situations; learn to think creatively as well as logically; assess the short and long-term implications of an issue; and generate a range of alternatives.

- Case studies can be presented in different formats: verbally, in writing, or as in-tray exercises, role-plays and video.

- Key stages in approaching case studies include reviewing the material, defining the problem(s), analysing the problem(s), formulating alternatives and presenting the results.

- Students are increasingly being asked to present case studies verbally so they need to master the presentation skills outlined in Chapter 7.

Tutorial

1. Use the checklist on page 158 to help you with your next case study:

   a) Review the material at least twice

   b) Clarify the main issues

   c) Use creative as well as logical approaches to problem-solving

   d) Review the material in Chapter 7 to help you make an effective presentation

2. Review the section on problem-solving on pages 151–157. Try to identify your main problem-solving style – is it logical, creative or a mixture of both?

3. If you are mainly a traditional logical thinker, review the comments on creative thinking and try to apply this approach when trying to solve your next problem.

Making presentations

One-minute overview

All the skills outlined so far play their part at different times in an individual's personal and career development, but the ability to relate to others in an interpersonal sense is the most constantly important and valuable.

All your knowledge, all your grasp of theory, all your general academic expertise would have a limited impact if it could not be conveyed to others in an interpersonal way. In both professional and academic contexts, effective presentations entail proficiency in a range of interpersonal skills.

Chapter 7 will help you develop an awareness of such skills and the processes involved. These include:
- good planning and preparation
- considering the audience
- providing structure
- using audio-visual aids
- rehearsing
- remembering
- aspects of speech
- non-verbal communication
- controlling nerves
- dealing with questions and interruptions.

7.1 Students and presentations

Students can experience presentations in different ways – for example, as part of an assignment, as an assignment in itself, or as part of a skills training programme. Students also view presentations in different ways. Some may see them purely as a means of gaining grades and regard them as an ordeal. Others, such as those who are in employment and attending courses part-time, recognise the value of presentations in terms of personal, social and career development and view them as a challenge. Making presentations enhances subject knowledge and develops crucial transferable personal skills, such as:

- making a case verbally

- appearing credible to others

- persuading others

- projecting confidence

- using non-verbal behaviour positively

- anticipating and overcoming negative responses

- using different media (such as diagrams and charts)

- dealing with questions.

Consequently, the skills associated with presentations will enable you to:

- capitalise on existing knowledge and expertise

- maximise input into seminars, meetings and other public performances

- improve your personal effectiveness at work and in a variety of social settings.

Focus points: effective presentations

Important aspects of effective presentation include the following:

- clarification of aims and objectives

- identification of the skills required

- effective research

- a clear structure

- considering the audience

- effective time management

- sound planning and preparation

- anticipating potential problems.

Note that the comments in this chapter relate to all kinds of presentations, not just those in an academic setting.

7.2 Planning and preparing

There is a strong link between effective planning and successful presentations. Although good planning in itself cannot guarantee success, it does increase the likelihood of the presentation being effective. Planning and preparation involve careful thought about the key presentation issues mentioned previously:

- identifying aims and objectives

- researching the topic

- the audience

- providing structure

- rehearsing.

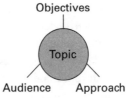

Figure 7.1 Planning and preparing ◀

Aims and objectives

Making a presentation usually involves more than just giving a talk. Whether intended or not, it invariably results in some sort of change. Simply giving information about a topic, for example, can result in knowledge being improved or awareness being raised. Consequently, the main considerations are as follows:

- What change is intended?

- What are the desired outcomes?

Presentation aims can range from wanting to inform and persuade through to increasing confidence, relieving anxiety or changing attitudes.

Key questions: aims and objectives

- What is the desired outcome?

- How can it be best achieved?

- How can I translate objectives into learning points?

- What are the main points I need to make?

- Is there an overall strategy? (e.g., inform, persuade, motivate)

- How can I check that my aims and objectives have been reached? (e.g., questions)

Researching the topic

Even if you are familiar with the topic, it is still important to gather plenty of information and to ensure that it comes from more than one source. This, of course, applies only to the planning stage. A presentation crowded with too much information will sink under its own weight. Many presenters prefer to have a lot of information to begin with, and then reduce this to key issues and points. Whatever your knowledge base, researching information will help you refresh your mind about what is relevant, identify the main points and order their sequence for logical delivery. There are many sources of information, ranging from personal notes to company, library and media sources (see Figure 7.2 for an illustration of some of these).

Figure 7.2 Researching the topic ▼

Whatever information is generated, you must remember that it will be best received if it is supported by evidence and appropriately linked to personal experience (avoid the repetition of dry facts where possible).

Checklist: research

- Research widely.

- Note the source.

- Identify a use for each item (such as handout, visual aid).

- Reduce information to key points.

- Support key points with evidence.

Considering the audience

In a manner of speaking the audience *is* the presentation. Whatever you wish to convey, no matter how important it is deemed to be, it will be of little use if the composition, needs and expectations of the audience are not considered. Therefore, the information given during a presentation should be based as much as possible on the information gained about the audience.

Researching the audience is essential to ensure that:

- aims and objectives are clarified

- the appropriate content is selected

- the presentation is pitched at the correct level

- boredom or offence is avoided

- adequate numbers are catered for.

Some of the key aspects of audience research are listed in Table 7.1.

Key aspects	Key questions
Background details	What is the age range? What is the general level of education/training? What kind of approach should be used? (e.g., clear examples) What degree of formality would be appropriate?
Indicative content	How much do they already know about the topic? How much do they need to know? How much additional knowledge is required? Are there any additional defined or potential needs?
Potential reaction	Have they been forced to attend? How objective are they? What is their likely attention span? How much information could they handle?

Table 7.1 Audience research

Other important aspects of audience research are the size of the audience and the nature of the venue. Size has implications in terms of, for example, equipment and handouts, but it can also influence your presentation style and general approach. Where the venue is concerned, it is advisable to:

- check for any potential noise or disruptions

- arrange the seating so that everyone in the audience is close enough to hear and see you easily

- check heating, ventilation, etc.

- sit where the audience sits – is the presenter's position suitable?

- check for blackout curtains if visual aids are to be used

- if a sound system is to be used, check that it is working effectively.

Checklist: audience

- Profile the audience: how might they differ in their needs and expectations?

- Clarify objectives: by the end of the presentation the audience should ...

- Plan and organise: good planning and organisation make the presenter appear confident, credible and professional.

- Identify the strategy: informing, persuading, changing attitudes, etc.

- Appreciate them: talk *to* them, not *at* them.

- Guide them: use signposts, such as 'first of all I will ..., then ...., and finally ...

- Be natural: be as natural as you can in the circumstances and avoid pretence.

- Be enthusiastic: enthusiasm like humour is infectious (but use humour carefully).

Providing structure

Once sufficient information has been generated by research, you need to provide some sort of structure. Structure is important because it enables the presenter to impart the information in a logical manner and it helps the audience follow the material presented. You should ensure that:

- the material is concise, clear and relevant

- there is a logical sequence

- interim summaries are provided (e.g., 'so far then ...')

- where appropriate, visual aids are used.

Structure can be viewed in the general sense of the three-stage approach (introduction, development and conclusion), and in the particular sense of a 'script' containing the sequence of the main points and supporting details.

1 **Introduction.** Along with the closing remarks, the opening statement is generally the more memorable part of a presentation and should be designed to capture the audience's attention. Unless you know the audience well, do not use jokes or startling comments. The best approach is to provide a clear outline of what the

presentation is about and state any limitations or restrictions. For example, if you prefer to leave questions to the end, this should be stated at the outset.

2 **Development.** While the style of the presenter can help concentration, the audience's attention may wander as the presentation continues. It is crucial, therefore, to develop the main points clearly and logically. You should provide linking words and phrases between points, use visual evidence where appropriate and provide interim summaries. Structuring comments in a certain way and repeating key words and phrases are valuable techniques for holding an audience during the development stage.

3 **Conclusion.** The end of a presentation provides an opportunity to refocus the audience on the key points. The audience has probably been listening to you for some time, so the conclusion must be as short and powerful as possible. Although handouts may be provided emphasising the main points, the aim of a good conclusion is to give the audience an impressive but simple mental package that they can take away with them and ponder.

An example of a simple but logical sequence is as follows:

Introduction	Opening pleasantries
	Statement of objectives
	Outline of presentation
	Mention of any limitations
Development	Development of key points
	Evidence for position adopted (if relevant)
	Coverage of opposing views (if necessary)
	Interim summaries (e.g., 'I would now like to examine...')
Conclusion	Final summary of main points

Weigh-up evidence

Restate/outline position

Conclude (thank them and invite questions)

Creating the 'script'

There are two ways of creating a detailed structure:

- writing the planned comments in full and then reducing them to key points

- starting with the selected key points and then adding the detail.

Both methods will improve your content knowledge (the more you read, the more you remember).

The word 'script' is used here in the planning sense. As discussed in section 7.5, reading a script is not making a presentation.

7.3 Audio-visual aids

Audio-visual aids enhance presentations. In some cases, they are essential to communicate complex information (e.g., pie charts to explain statistics).

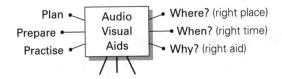

*Figure 7.3
Audio-visual
aids*

Focus points: audio visual aids

Audio-visual aids can:

- provide focal points for the presentation

- reinforce key issues

- clarify complex matters

- help the audience to remember

- make the presenter look professional

- take the pressure off the presenter.

Although audio-visual aids help illustrate and reinforce the presenter's comments, a careful balance must be maintained between the aids and the comments. If visual aids are not planned and used selectively, the focus shifts from the presenter to the aid in an unbalanced way. The aid then becomes the presentation. Visual aids also play an important role as a timing device. They introduce pauses into a presentation, giving the audience a rest from the presenter's voice and allowing them to reflect on the points made. A range of audio-visual aids is available and the most common are:

- flipchart

- whiteboard

- overhead projector

- computer-linked projector

- tape or slide projector

- video tapes and films

- tape recorder

- models and samples.

The overhead projector

The overhead projector (OHP) is probably the most common and popular visual aid. Its advantages and disadvantages are listed in Table 7.2.

An OHP is simple to use, but it requires practice to maximise its impact. Some presenters prefer to show everything on the transparency at once, and then add information related to each separate point. (Merely repeating what is written on the transparency seriously undermines the credibility of the presenter.) Others believe that this is distracting and confusing for the audience. They maintain that gradually revealing the information allows time for the audience to absorb and reflect on the information. With experience, transparencies can be read without losing too much eye contact with the audience. However, you must be careful not to obscure the audience's view of the screen. You must also keep checking that the projected image is lined up with the screen, not the ceiling.

Advantages	Disadvantages
Provides a valuable focal point	Transparencies may look scruffy
Simple to use	Presenter may stand in front of screen
Facilitates control of the 'message'	Too much information on transparency
Useful as a memory aid	The OHP is left on after use (distraction)
Powerful impact	Too many transparencies are used
Professional image if used well	The OHP takes over the presentation

▲
*Table 7.2
The overhead
projector*

Checklist: OHP

- Question the need for a transparency (what is it going to achieve?).

- Plan where the OHP is going to be used.

- Prepare transparencies carefully (use a clipboard and ruled paper, or type them in a larger font).

- Make sure you have your transparencies in the order in which you are going to show them.

- Don't put too much information on one transparency.

- Use different colours to highlight key points.

- Where possible, use images rather than text.

- Avoid detailed information such as statistics (it is better to use a handout).

- Don't use too many transparencies.

- Number the transparencies.

- Use the bullet-point approach (key words and phrases only).

- Don't just read what is written on the transparency (give additional information).

- Allow time for the audience to absorb the information.

- Switch off the OHP after use.

Note that many of the above points also apply to computer-linked projectors.

It is important to remember the different ways in which information can be presented:

- Contrasts can greatly enhance understanding of the overall situation.

- Devices such as bar charts and pie charts help the audience to make comparisons and understand complicated information (such as statistics).

- Diagrams, flowcharts and illustrations are particularly useful for aiding understanding of a sequence of events.

Checklist: writing during a presentation
Make sure you:

- have spare chalk and pens handy

- don't stand in front of the screen

- check the size of your writing (view it from the back of the room)

- write first, then comment (doing both together may be impressive, but it can confuse the audience)

- outline any diagrams in pencil first (flip charts).

7.4 Rehearsing

Even confident presenters appreciate the importance of rehearsing, particularly when adding new aspects to existing material, or if the presentation has significant ramifications. No matter how effectively you plan and prepare, the potential impact of the presentation cannot be accurately assessed without a rehearsal. Rehearsing is especially useful for:

- checking timing

- editing material

- appraising audio-visual aids

- evaluating overall structure

- confirming where linking words or phrases are necessary

- pronouncing difficult words

- identifying bad habits (oral/non-verbal).

Increased confidence = improved delivery

Checklist: rehearsal

- Are you familiar with the equipment?

- Is the material effectively edited?

- Are the visual aids satisfactory?

- Do you have appropriate memory aids?

- Have you noted particular aspects of time?

- Have you identified difficult words/phrases/material?

- Have you noted negative verbal/non-verbal habits?

7.5 Delivery

Poor presenting behaviour can be categorised as follows:

- **The Racer:** will get to end no matter what

- **The Rambler:** moves from one point to another with no clear structure

- **The Rambo:** overenthusiastic, attacks the script and almost does the same to the audience (uncontrolled non-verbal behaviour)

- **The Reader:** glued to his or her notes, resulting in a dry, boring delivery

- **The Rector:** preaches at the audience

- **The Rookie:** inexperienced and shows it; appears a nervous wreck

- **The Rumbler:** rumbles along in a monotone, almost inaudible voice

  Effective delivery comprises several key components:

- **Remembering:** impressing the audience with a clear command of the facts (with minimal aids)

- **Communication style:** command of language, exuding trust, credibility, and inspiring confidence

- **Personality traits:** conveying enthusiasm, warmth and energy; the ability to develop a good relationship with the audience

- **Non-verbal behaviour:** deliberate, positive use of non-verbal behaviour to support speech and hold the audience

- **Tone of voice:** using volume and tone to cue, emphasise and create atmosphere

- **Timing:** using audio-visual aids, pauses and silence to maximise effect

It is better to distribute handouts at the end of the presentation. Giving them out during it can have a negative effect on your delivery and distract the audience.

Remembering

Closely associated with nervousness, failure to remember is probably one of the most feared aspects of making presentations. Relying solely on memory (helped by minimal aids) is a method favoured by some presenters, but as discussed in section 7.2, it has drawbacks:

- it requires significant concentration and expertise

- important points can be missed

- the structure of the presentation can be unclear

- the potential for disaster is greatly increased.

Many presenters memorise the main presentation stages and key points. This memory base can be supplemented by a variety of audio-visual aids such as flipcharts and cue cards. These aids can be used subtly by experienced presenters, but inexperienced presenters should take care with aids such as cue cards. The most effective way of using cue cards is to present them in a forthright manner, thus creating the impression that they are a natural part of the presentation. Sensible precautions should be taken when using cue cards (as some presenters have discovered to their cost):

- write only on one side

- use highlighting and spacing to aid reading

- punch a hole in the corner of each card and secure with string or treasury tags

- use the key point approach

- number each card.

Aspects of speech

Important though the different areas relating to delivery are, the main method of communication in presentations is the human voice. Speaking effectively means following a number of separate but related strategies (see Table 7.3).

Articulate	Speak as clearly as you can under the circumstances; uncontrolled nerves can cause you to be inarticulate.
Pronounce properly	No matter how good your command of English is, various words can cause problems with respect to pronunciation. Where this is likely to be the case, try to find other words to replace them (use a thesaurus) or break the word down and rehearse.
Vary pitch and tone	Nothing is more boring than listening to a person speaking in a monotone. Try to make your voice more interesting.
Enunciate	Add emphasis to certain words and phrases; for example: – 'I think this is important' – 'I *think* this is important' – 'I think *this* is important'.
Repeat	As with written work, repetition must be used selectively and sparingly. Repetition is particularly useful where inspiration is required: '*We* have the ability to succeed, *we* have the resolve to succeed, *we* will succeed' (use of emphasis and personalisation as well as repetition, i.e. 'we').
Project	Wherever they sit, everyone must be able to hear you; project your voice. Voice volume must be appropriate for the room and the size of the audience; it must also not be too forceful or overbearing. Changes in volume can be used for emphasis, providing links and signalling transitions.
Pause	Timed correctly, it can create an air of expectancy and focus attention. It is important to consider using pauses: – at the start of the presentation (especially if full attention is not given) – before making a key point (the build-up approach) – after giving a complex piece of information (allows the audience 'brain time') – towards the end of the presentation (aids consideration of the key issues).

Table 7.3
Aspects of speech

Improving aspects of speech such as articulation entails exercises like:

- shaping the words more than you might do normally (use the lips more)

- increasing the emphasis on consonants

- slowing down your speaking speed

- using short pauses, especially between difficult words or phrases.

Other exercises, such as control of breathing, use of the lips, throat and so on, are important supporting strategies in achieving maximum vocal effect.

Focus points: aspects of speech

- Use simple and clear words, phrases and sentences.

- Informing is more important than impressing (be economical in your use of words).

- Deliver in a style that is appropriate to the audience.

- If technical terms have to be used, explain them briefly (even experts may need reminding, but don't patronise).

- Avoid jargon, slang and 'in-words'.

- Avoid pet words and phrases (such as 'obviously', 'quite apparent').

- Use techniques such as emphasis and pauses (but carefully consider where).

- Vary pitch and tone.

- Speak loud enough to be heard (but volume must be appropriate to room and audience size).

- If you tend to speak quickly, make a causcious effort to slow down.

Non-verbal communication

Although *what* the presenter says is important, *how* the information is delivered is crucial in terms of supporting the presenter's overall message. Some aspects of *how* have already been described, but the significance of non-verbal communication (NVC) should not be underestimated.

Although voice is important, people communicate with their whole body.

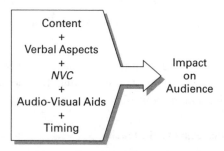

NVC includes all the body language that people consciously or unconsciously convey. The term non-verbal behaviour (NVB) is sometimes used to denote body language that the individual is unaware of, but NVC is the generally accepted description of this important form of human communicating behaviour.

When people meet (especially for the first time), whether they are conscious of the fact or not, they are communicating, receiving and interpreting a range of non-verbal signals such as facial expressions (particularly eye contact), gestures and various other aspects of personal appearance. It is worth remembering that as well as supporting what the presenter says, NVC can also undermine or even contradict what is stated verbally. This is the uncontrolled aspect of NVC, sometimes referred to as, 'leakage' (in spite of the person's attempts at control, contradictory signals leak out).

Facial expression

Most people understand what most facial expressions mean (happiness, sadness, fear, surprise and so on). Experienced presenters are very much aware that facial movements involving smiles, nods and eye contact reveal attitude. For example, smiles which are appropriately given and well-timed can demonstrate that the presenter is human and has a sense of humour; they are vital for 'unfreezing' the audience and building a good relationship.

Focus points: eye contact

Eye contact is crucial for:

- confirming the presenter's confidence
- building a bond with the audience
- holding the audience's attention
- reinforcing key points
- supporting the credibility of the message.

Try to avoid:

- concentrating on individuals sitting at the front
- ignoring members of the audience at the back or sides of the room
- letting eye contact turn into a gaze.

Posture

You may find it difficult to control your natural posture, particularly when you are anxious or under pressure. Try to adopt a position that is as natural as possible in the circumstances, but manages to avoid those elements of posture that may create an unfavourable impression. It is important that you:

- squarely and confidently face the audience (especially at the beginning)
- avoid slouched positions where possible (even if trying to communicate informality)
- don't pace up and down as this may unsettle the audience (and seriously affects posture)
- avoid gripping the lectern (this may transmit a wooden appearance)

- breathe deeply (but subtly), as this relaxes the body and helps control posture.

Gestures

Although gestures can be made with most parts of the body, the hands are generally the most expressive (and distracting). Pointing to visuals and supporting speech are examples of positive gestures that help build a relationship with the audience. Conversely, too many gestures can convey an almost comical impression which undermines both the message and the presenter. Audiences are quite capable of decoding involuntary as well as intended NVC, and gestures are less subtle than some other forms of NVC. Consequently, a careful balance must be struck between overuse of gestures and the adoption of an almost lifeless appearance.

Focus points: NVC

- Clothes send messages about the presenter – dress appropriately.

- Adopt a confident posture (don't slouch or appear wooden).

- Avoid pacing up and down.

- Smiles are invaluable for developing rapport (but they must appear natural).

- Controlled nodding can be used to regulate feedback from the audience.

- Maintain regular eye contact with the audience.

- Keep gestures to a minimum.

Nerves

It is possible to be well prepared and confident, yet still nervous. Indeed, most presenters feel some degree of nervousness before a presentation. This is not a bad thing,

since it helps concentrate the mind and prevents the
presenter from becoming overconfident. So nerves keep the
presenter alert and tuned-in to the audience. Nerves are
often more of a problem before the presentation than during
it, and this is one reason why they usually diminish as the
presentation continues. For some, however, nerves remain a
serious problem. Table 7.4 lists some potential problems and
recommended strategies for dealing with them.

Table 7.4
Nerves
▼

Potential problem	Recommended strategy
Poor audience reaction	Keep thinking: 'I've prepared well and rehearsed'
	Practise positive NVC to develop rapport
	Commit the opening lines to memory
	Speak to the audience
Memory loss	Consider the range of memory aids
	Use the memory aid you prefer
	Plan any visuals so as to provide 'thinking time'
	Keep back-up notes close at hand
Getting the sequence wrong	Avoid complicated sequences if possible
	Use a visual for prioritised lists (complex ones on handouts)
	Don't panic (only you know the exact sequence)
	Use a comment like, 'at this point, I am not referring to these in any particular order'
Speech problems	Always have a glass of water at hand (but sip slowly)
	Slow down
	Breathe deeply
	Think of the key words or concept
Equipment malfunctions	Don't panic, make light of the problem
	Plan for problems: keep spares if possible (e.g., bulbs for OHP, stand-by video cassette and recorder)
	Use an additional method for key facts (e.g., handouts)
	View the problem as an opportunity to impress, e.g., 'these things sometimes happen, I will now use the flipchart/handout to reinforce the key points contained in the video I was going to show'

Focus points: nerves

Remember that:

- feeling nervous is natural (and to a certain extent, necessary)

- using personal relaxation strategies before presentations (e.g., listening to music) often helps

- you can identify personal symptoms of nervousness and develop strategies to overcome them

- you can reduce any feelings of nervousness during the presentation by breathing deeply and concentrating on the task in hand

- if you feel confident you'll appear confident.

- above all, don't panic.

Dealing with questions

Because questions are unpredictable, they are difficult to prepare for. However, as with all aspects of a presentation, the key to success is effective planning. One of the fundamental planning issues is whether to allow questions during the presentation or at the end. Another important element in planning is the amount of time allocated to questions. It is not possible to anticipate questions exactly, of course, but it may be possible to anticipate, in a broad sense, the type and range of questions the audience might ask. Again, a crucial factor is the presenter's topic knowledge. Here are some examples of questions that presenters should ask themselves:

- What are the key issues?

- Are there any problem issues?

- What issues have had to be left out? (time constraint)

- What questions would I find the most difficult to answer? (more homework required)

- What questions would I ask if I were in the audience?

Key points: dealing with questions

Listen carefully. In addition to hearing the actual words, perceptive listening may be required to identify particular views or assumptions that may lie behind a particular question.

Strategy: Practise active listening (that is, listen for meaning as well as the actual words used).

Equal opportunity. Don't allow one member of the audience to hog question time. Not only is this frustrating for other members, but the guilty party is using your time to make a mini-presentation of their own.

Strategy: Use the time factor to move on. For example: 'I'm sorry, but I have to move on as time is running out'.

Keep control. Some questioners may not only be hostile to the presenter, they may also be hostile to each other, using the presentation to score points.

Strategy: a) Use the time factor mentioned above

b) Invite questions from other members

c) Threaten to terminate question time (actually do this as a last resort)

Difficult questions. If you don't know the answer to a question, say so. If you feel you can give a reasonable answer but need thinking time, play for time. If the question will put you in a 'no win' situation, seek to avoid answering it (politicians do it all the time).

Strategy: a) Be honest if you don't know the answer

b) If you do know the answer, you may wish to play for time by asking the questioner to explain what they mean

c) If you wish to gauge the strength of feeling about an issue, ask how many others feel the same

d) If you don't wish to answer a question directly, throw it to the audience and then summarise

e) If you are forced to answer, the best course is to empathise and give a neutral reply. For example: 'While I understand the views behind the question are valid, perhaps the best course of action is ...'

Coping with interruptions

Despite the ground rules set, questions or comments may not come at the requested time. So you must have a strategy to deal with interruptions. Indeed, how this is accomplished can seriously affect your credibility; it is also often an indication of your self-confidence and experience. Although most audiences resent interruptions and hostile questions (and are therefore on your side), you should have a variety of responses ready to deal with such situations. Above all, you must remain calm and not allow a member of the audience to defeat you.

Some examples of responses are as follows:

- Use humour (but don't patronise).

- Make a positive response – for example, 'I'm glad you've asked this question because it gives me the opportunity to ...'

- 'Kill them with kindness', highlight their lack of grace by demonstrating your tolerance, patience and good manners.

- Outflank them – for example, 'If you all wish me to deal with this question now I will, but perhaps you might wish me to continue as agreed, and outline the key points first?' (use of non-verbal communication such as eye contact is crucial in this case).

Focus points: question time

- Seek feedback if necessary.

- Decide when questions are to be asked (make this clear to the audience).

- Develop a range of strategies to deal with potential problems.

- Keep control of the audience.

- Handle interruptions courteously and professionally (but firmly).

- Don't waffle (be honest if you don't know the answer).

Summary

- Presentations are crucial for maximising other skills.

- Presentations involve more than just giving a talk, they can include objectives such as behavioural change.

- Planning and preparation are essential for success.

- The audience need 'signposts' and an easy-to-follow structure.

- Audio-visual aids can reinforce key points and help take the pressure off the presenter.

- Rehearsing pays dividends, giving you increased confidence and improving your performance.

- Effective delivery entails a good grasp of content, using the voice to maximum effect and adopting positive aspects of non-verbal communication.

- Memory can be improved by using a range of techniques such as flipcharts, the overhead projector and cue cards.

- Speaking effectively means following a number of separate but related strategies; for example, varying pitch and tone, and adding emphasis to certain words or phrases.

- A key element in how the information is delivered and perceived is non-verbal communication; aspects such as eye contact are crucial in this respect.

- Nervousness can be alleviated through rehearsal and deep-breathing exercises.

- Dealing with questions can be less stressful if you use strategies such as throwing the question back at the questioner or the audience and then summarising.

Tutorial

1 Determine the overall strategy of your next presentation. For example, do you intend to impartially inform, persuade, enthuse? Identify what impact this has on aspects such as speech, opening comments, conclusions.

2 The voice is a key factor in presentation success. Make your voice sound more interesting by using a tape recorder to practise changes in pitch, tone, speed and so on.

3 Assess the effectiveness of your delivery. Use a video camera or the help of friends. An appraisal checklist might be useful:

	Examples	Comments
Introduction	statement of objectives	
Voice	clarity, speed, tone	
Content	relevant, well-organised	
Structure	clear logical order	
Transitions	linking words/phrases	
Time	too long? too short?	
Non-verbal behaviour	eye contact	
Audio-visual aids	clarity, number	
Memory aids	effectively used?	
Summary	key points re-emphasised	

8 Revision and exams

One-minute overview

Even the most capable and conscientious student is understandably anxious at the thought of months, indeed years of study, being assessed in the relatively short period of the examination. A common fear among students is not that they do not know the facts related to their subject areas, but, given the constrained time period of the exam, that they may not recall the facts comprehensively, in enough detail and in the logical, structured manner required.

Since aspects of revision and general technique appear to be crucial to exam success, Chapter 8 will:

- raise awareness about the various revision strategies available
- reinforce the importance of regular and intensified revision
- emphasise the techniques available for improving recall
- highlight the different types of exams and common mistakes
- consider the strategies that can be adopted to combat stress
- offer advice on how to prepare for and tackle exams.

It is strongly recommended that other sections relevant to this chapter are reviewed again, such as planning and organising, note taking, essay writing and case studies.

8.1 Revision

One important distinction between revision and exams is that revision is largely content-related (the *what* – trying to remember as many facts as possible), whereas exams are chiefly strategy and technique-related (the *how*). The ability to recall key facts is of course crucial in exams, but this alone is not enough. What is also required is the ability to apply, structure and evaluate such facts under pressure – hence the emphasis on strategy and technique.

Research indicates that although our learning curve actually rises shortly after our brain processes information, without any revision we can lose up to 80% of the content within 24 hours. The message is clear: the more regularly you revise, the more you remember.

Figure 8.1 The benefits of revision ▼

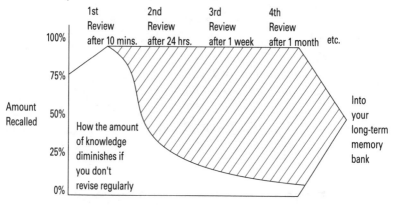

Revision is a process composed of several elements:

- updating, editing and critically evaluating notes

- refreshing your memory by reading your notes regularly

- using the brain's power to retrieve information and process it (such as in a self-test); this activity develops understanding as well as memory.

Helping the brain to remember

People remember things in different ways, and each individual has to find the most appropriate and efficient method for them. A significant point in relation to study is that it is not so much a case of forgetting what you have learned, but that you are unable to recall it. There is an important difference.

Being unable to recall information implies that with the aid of appropriate methods you might be able to improve your ability to recall and retrieve. Research supports the common-sense view that organised and meaningful material is easier to remember. Material in visual form is also easier to commit to memory and recall. Therefore, the process of memorising is greatly facilitated if the material is (or is made to be):

- **Organised:** organising and structuring material makes it easier to remember

- **Reduced:** reduce the material or data to more manageable learning units and key words and phrases (e.g., 'crib cards')

- **Visual:** the more visual the material is, the easier it is to commit to memory and recall (e.g., pattern notes)

- **Immediate:** the more recent the memory, the easier it is to recall

- **Repeated:** the more you repeat the facts to be remembered, the more you will learn

- **Rhymed:** for example, 'i before e, except after c'

- **Listened to:** use a tape recorder or personal hi-fi to review material (especially before going to sleep)

- **Significant:** the more meaningful the material is, and the more it is related to existing knowledge, the greater is the amount of material you will recall

- **Understandable:** it is very difficult to remember something if you don't fully understand it. Learning by simply repeating facts has a limited use

- **Enjoyable:** people learn best when they enjoy what they are doing; learning should not be a dismal process

- **Linked:** look for links between information

- **Tested:** self-testing is crucial for enhancing memory (what can you recall about this chapter so far?)

- **Rested:** take regular breaks between study sessions; do not study for longer than 40–60 minutes without a break

Other activities are also necessary to maximise the brain's ability to recall information. An important one is discussion, which:

- tests your knowledge

- forces you to critically evaluate knowledge

- can bring new insights

- develops the skills of presentation and argument.

Mnemonics

Mnemonics are devices for aiding the memory, and there are several different types. The most common is the acronym, where the first letters of the items to be remembered are used to form a word, for example, ASS (Awareness-raising, Skills development and Support). Another involves developing a rhyme or saying which also uses the first letters of the item to be remembered. Mnemonics, therefore, depend on:

- the power of association

- a novel or meaningful word or phrase

- the significance of the word or phrase for the particular individual.

For some reason, this powerful method for improving memory seems not to be used as often as it could be after the earlier years of schooling.

The following mnemonics can be applied to study skills in general:

ASK	KISS	GUEST	SUS IT
Attitude	**K**eep	**G**alvanise your thoughts	**S**elect the key points
Skills	**I**t	**U**nderstand the main points	**U**nderstand, then memorise
Knowledge	**S**hort and **S**imple	**E**xamine all the evidence	**S**ystematise – work to a system
		Support points with evidence	**I**nnovate – think laterally
		Try a rough draft first	**T**est your knowledge

As mentioned earlier, remembering facts and details by rote without really understanding them does not increase your knowledge in a meaningful way. So understanding is central to the revision process. When you understand you:

● determine how the information contributes to the overall pattern of explanation

● conceptualise, theorise and look for implications

● don't just accept and present information as you find it, but interpret, analyse and develop it.

However, there are times when rote learning is necessary. For instance, when all the recommended strategies for aiding memory have been tried and found wanting, or when the material does not fall into a particular pattern or meaningful whole. It would be difficult, for example, to create an acronym from SMTWTFS (the days of the week). This is why rhyming and rote learning become necessary (for example, '30 days hath September ...').

The link between study, revision and assessment can be viewed as a cyclical process (see Figure 8.2). First, detailed notes are taken (say, from a lecture). Then these notes are reduced to more manageable units for study and revision purposes. Lastly, the process is reversed and the skeleton units are built up and developed.

*Figure 8.2
The cyclical
process of
study and
revision*
▶

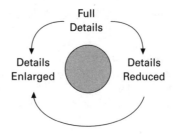

This overall sequence of recording, reducing and enlarging information, linked to regular revision, means that the retention of subject knowledge is increased.

The reduction of information is an important element of revision and the cyclical process illustrated in Figure 8.2 is linked to various activities. For many students, these activities take the following form:

1 The various pieces of the original source material are collated.

2 After careful examination, these primary sources are reduced to subject summary sheets.

3 These summary sheets are reduced to 'crib cards' (a memory aid consisting of the basic key points). It is important that the original source notes or other items are kept for reference purposes, since crucial facts can be omitted at the crib card stage.

*Figure 8.3
From source
material to crib
cards*
▶

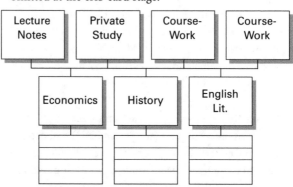

Note. The prime purpose of crib cards is to make the revision process more manageable, not to aid simplistic repetition (crib cards are no substitute for understanding).

Table 8.1 lists potential problems and solutions in approaches to revision.

Potential problem	Potential solution
Deciding when to start	Effective recall depends upon regular revision. When revision should be intensified depends on the individual, but 6–8 weeks before exams is generally a good rule of thumb.
Identifying what to revise	Develop a revision plan based on the syllabus, subject-tutor advice, relevant notes and previous exam papers.
My worst topic is ...	Allocate more time to subjects you have difficulty with, but not to the detriment of other subjects (adopt a balanced approach to revision).
Knowing when I can revise	Create a detailed but flexible revision timetable containing the maximum amount of revision hours you can realistically cope with. Such a timetable should include rest and reward periods (e.g., listening to music; an evening out with friends).
Knowing what to practise	This depends on the exam format, and could include: essay-type answers, multiple choice responses, case studies etc. A useful strategy is to set yourself a mock exam.

Table 8.1
Approaches to revision: problems and solutions

Revision is not

Reading material a few days before the exam

Hoping to 'cram' at the last moment

Relying on some sort of super memory

Leaving things in the 'lap of the gods'

Trying to memorise chunks of material

Studying when you feel like it

Revision is

Adopting an overall structured approach

Increasing study 6–8 weeks before the exam

Using a variety of revision methods

Setting yourself clear and achievable goals

Reducing material to manageable units

Using time management techniques

8.2 Exams

Types of exams and common mistakes

Exams fall into three main categories:

- recalling knowledge (the 'all I know about ...' approach)

- the application of knowledge (for example, problem-solving)

- practical skills tests (associated with vocational or training situations).

Knowledge-based tests

Although you may not be expected to demonstrate more than the possession of knowledge, if time and ability permits, there is no reason why you should confine yourself to simply recounting facts or data. However, as with all exams, the primary objective is to answer the question set. Knowledge-based tests can be approached more effectively by:

- revising thoroughly

- using examples where possible

- creating meaningful wholes rather than just providing unrelated pieces of information

- emphasising key points

- highlighting similarities and differences.

An increasingly familiar format for testing knowledge is the multiple-choice question paper. One of the problems associated with this format is that students may become overconfident (before, during or after the exam). They forget for example, that:

- some potential answers can appear very similar

- the correct answer to a sequence of questions might always appear in the same position (e.g., response (d) –

this can confuse a candidate who is not sure of the answer)

● some questions can be in stages.

You should also be careful about other things, such as 'easy' answers occurring near the beginning of the multiple-choice paper. When this happens, it often makes the unwary candidate overconfident. Such exam paper formats can cause problems if you are not sure of the facts (particularly if certain questions occur when you are beginning to tire).

Applying-knowledge tests

In this form of test, the important thing is not just the selection of appropriate forms of knowledge, but the use to which this is put. In other words, how knowledge is applied. Various strategies can be adopted, such as:

- self-testing before the exam
- reading the question carefully
- considering all the possible consequences
- identifying the various parts of the questions
- following any instructions precisely (e.g., 'analyse').

Question Analysis Technique (review page 107)

Applying-knowledge tests often expect an essay-type answer. While consideration will be given to the fact that the essay has been written under exam conditions, key elements are still expected (for example, subject knowledge and understanding; an evaluation of the relevant ideas, theories and concepts; logical argument and structure; some attempt to go beyond mere fact-giving). If you cannot remember all the advice given on essay writing in Chapter 4, before tackling the question at least try to remember the sequence illustrated in Figure 8.4.

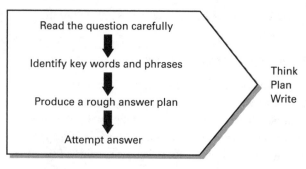

Figure 8.4
Essay-writing
sequence
▶

Practical skill tests

The emphasis in these tests is usually on producing a piece of work within a given time, and candidates face the usual exam dilemma of quality versus time. Students facing a practical skills test should:

- review previous test papers

- check the regulations (e.g., are you allowed more material if you make a mistake?)

- check if any previous test examples or models are available for inspection

- verify exactly how long the test is

- if possible, practise a similar test piece under the same time constraint

- ascertain what facilities (if any) are provided at the test venue

- make a checklist of the tools and equipment you require

- think positively (e.g., 'I have produced this piece/conducted this process many times before').

Focus points: common exam mistakes

Some of the commonest exam mistakes are:

- choosing questions too quickly

- not answering the question set

- straying from the point

- poor time management (e.g., spending too long on one
  question and thus not completing all the questions)

- not providing enough evidence

- giving only a partial account (bias)

- neglecting key concepts/theories

- failure to demonstrate academic skills (e.g., critical
  analysis)

- poor presentation (e.g., no clear structure, not enough
  paragraphs, illegible handwriting).

8.3 Coping with nerves

The title of this section implies that nervousness or stress is
always a feature of exams. Apart from a fortunate few, this is
often the case. As noted in Chapter 7, a degree of
nervousness can improve exam performance. However, as
the extract on page 92 verifies, anxiety about exams can
reach such a point that it not only becomes problematic, but
the student becomes ill. One way of tackling this is to
develop stress-reducing strategies like those indicated below.

Apathy. This could be the result of overconfidence ('no
problem') as well as too much stress ('I can't cope'). If it is
not dealt with, it can have serious repercussions.

Strategy: a) Develop a general action plan (be proactive).

b) Create a revision timetable with regular
(achievable) goals.

Lack of concentration. Although this could be the result of
stress, it could also reflect lack of confidence. Unresolved,
this is a major problem; if you cannot concentrate, you
cannot study, revise or pass exams.

Strategy: a) Set yourself a specific target to be achieved
against a reduced time constraint of 20–25
minutes. Such an activity could entail
summarising or producing cue cards.

   b) Build upon strategy (a) above by extending the time period to 40–60 minutes and tackling a more difficult task (such as a self-test).

Desperation (too many exams). Being overawed, in the first instance, by the number of exams to be coped with is to be expected at certain times; it is an understandable reaction to a stressful period. This could also indicate lack of self-confidence.

Strategy: a) Get things into perspective by viewing each exam as a series of objectives to be achieved.

   b) Intensify revision at an early stage to boost confidence.

   c) Reappraise your planning and organisation.

Sleeplessness. It is not unusual in stress-related situations like exams or job interviews (where the brain is working overtime) to have difficulty in sleeping some time before the event. Importantly, the question is the degree to which this is occurring.

Strategy: a) Plenty of physical exercise and sport if health permits (you must be physically fit); walking is a good alternative.

   b) Relaxation activities such as controlled breathing (e.g., breathe in, hold your breath briefly, and breathe out slowly).

   c) If the problem persists, consult your doctor.

Panic attacks. These generally occur either immediately before the exam or during it (or both). Whatever the circumstances, panic attacks need to be countered immediately by logical, constructive thinking and concentration on the task in hand. (Because of the irrationality of panic attacks, this approach may need several attempts.) In extreme cases, medical attention may be required.

Strategy: a) If the panic occurs before the exam, think positively, for example, 'I have passed exams before, I will pass this one' (repeat this if necessary until the panic subsides).

b) If the panic occurs during the exam (for example, if you have a 'mental block'), quickly implement revision strategies such as, 'Think, Plan, Write'.

Checklist: exam nerves

- Try to identify exactly what is causing the anxiety (for example, use pattern notes).

- Be perceptive, identify early signs of abnormal anxiety (such as mood swings, loss of appetite).

- Develop your own stress-management techniques (such as sport, music, controlled breathing).

- Identify specific strategies to overcome particular anxiety-causing situations (such as memory techniques to prevent mental blocks).

- Be determined (for example, 'there is no way exam nerves are going to spoil my performance').

- Reduce time spent waiting outside the exam venue (use this time for a last review of crib cards and boosting self-confidence).

- Don't let panic thoughts linger, dispel them by concentrating on the task in hand.

- View exams as a challenge, not a threat.

- If nerves continue to be a problem, see your tutor and seek medical advice.

8.4 Exam preparation

As well as intensified revision, exam preparation usually involves the following:

Reviewing the syllabus	Tutors normally allocate periods of revision during which likely topics and how they should be tackled, will be discussed. It is vital that you attend these, and ask your subject tutors' advice about any aspects of the syllabus which may be causing anxiety. It is a good idea to confer with your study group or fellow students. They may have particular expertise or interest in a specific part of the syllabus. As stated earlier, it is important not to concentrate solely on parts of the syllabus with which you feel comfortable (to the detriment of subject areas you may be less strong on).
Studying previous papers	As many students have found to their cost, question spotting can be a fruitless activity. The anticipated questions may not come up, or the way they are phrased can completely alter the approach you had planned for. Therefore, it is best to: – use old exam papers primarily to practise answering technique – revise on a topic basis rather than specific questions – again, consult your tutor.
Writing model answers	Although relying solely on previous questions for revision purposes has been criticised, practising model answers to enhance technique is an effective pre-exam strategy. As in revision as a whole, methods such as pattern notes and mnemonics are useful in preparing and remembering the structure of model answers.
Exam administration	Well before the exam, check: – the time and place (exact location) of the exam – that you have your candidate number – that you have all the equipment required.

8.5 The exam itself

Checking the paper	Ensure that the paper is the correct one for the subject and course; mistakes can happen. Exam paper instructions usually indicate how much time you have; the number of questions that must be answered; the marks allocated to each question (or parts of a question). It is important to follow any instructions precisely and:

	– check if there are any compulsory questions – check if questions have to be answered in a specific way, particularly in the case of multiple-choice questions – carefully follow any instructions for changing answers.
Choosing questions	Some exam boards allocate time for reading the paper. Whether or not this is the case, time spent appraising the paper will pay dividends. Select the answers to be attempted with care and prioritise them. Tackling the question you believe to be the easiest first will save time and increase confidence. Check the selected answers again to verify that you can answer them all completely.
Answering questions	Manage time effectively: Divide the time equally between the number of questions to be answered. Allocate the time in proportion to the marks stipulated (where the question is divided into parts). Leave problem aspects (but return to them later). Analyse the question and follow any instructions, e.g., 'discuss' (review pages 107–111). Plan the answers, and try to recall any memory aid previously used in order to structure a rough outline. Stick to the question set and where possible give examples, use key words/phrases, provide evidence. The more questions attempted, the greater are the potential marks. If the time allocated to a particular question is up (and it is not nearly finished), leave it and try to return to it later; quickly scribble any notes to enable the answer to be completed. If you are unable to complete a question before the time is up, it is advisable to provide a 'completion plan' (a list of key points to indicate what would have been covered).
Handwriting	Examiners are not unreasonable in expecting handwriting to be legible. No matter how legible your handwriting is, it will often deteriorate as the exam progresses; poor handwriting can result in poor marks. Even if it means slowing down, make an effort to write legibly. Crossings out should be neat, and there shouldn't be any over-writing.

| Final check | Check all answers for clarity, omissions, misspellings etc.
Ensure that completion outlines have been provided for any unfinished questions.
Verify that your name is on the answer book and any separate pages, and that the questions attempted have been clearly identified. |

Critical success factors in the exam itself are related to:

- the way questions are selected
- planning how the selected questions should be answered
- demonstrating academic skills
- and good time management.

Above all, don't:

- be overconfident
- leave the exam early
- hold an inquest.

Checklist: exams

When preparing for exams, it is a good idea to:

- review the syllabus
- seek advice and guidance from subject tutors
- intensify revision well before the exam
- revise on a topic basis, don't question-spot
- self-test to improve performance
- adopt stress-management techniques
- read the paper thoroughly and with care.

During the exam, you should:

- manage your time effectively
- choose the questions carefully and prioritise them

- analyse the question for key words and phrases

- produce a rough outline plan for each answer

- emphasise key points and support with evidence

- regularly check the question title to keep on track

- provide completion plans where necessary

- pay attention to structure and presentation

- ensure all questions have been answered

- make a final check for errors.

We all have different learning curves and become proficient in different things at different times. In many cases, exams do not come when people are at the peak of the curve. The most you can do is your best – no one can ask more.

Summary

- Although both revision and exams are content-related, strategy and technique play a crucial role during exams.

- Regular revision enhances study and increases memory retention.

- Organised and meaningful material is easier to recall; material in audio or visual form is also easier to commit to memory and recall.

- Mnemonics are excellent for improving memory and depend on the power of association, a novel or meaningful phrase, and the meaning and significance of the word or phrase for the particular individual.

- The reduction of information is a key element of revision and is linked to activities such as gathering primary sources, reducing these to summary sheets and, lastly, transferring the key points to crib cards.

- Exams fall into three main categories: recalling knowledge; the application of knowledge; and practical skills tests.

- Common exam mistakes include choosing questions too quickly, not answering the question set and straying from the point.

- Although a degree of nervousness can be beneficial, exam anxiety may reach such a level that students can become ill. Strategies to overcome nervousness include: identifying exactly what is causing the anxiety; being positive; using stress-management techniques.

- As well as intensified revision, exam preparation includes activities such as revising the syllabus, studying previous exam papers and writing model answers.

- Candidates should not be overconfident, leave the exam early, or hold an inquest afterwards.

Tutorial

1 Regular, planned revision is the best way to improve recall. Using your revision plan, determine:

   a) how much you have revised in the last week(s) or month

   b) how this revision time has been allocated across the various subjects

   c) what (if any) information has been reduced to a key point system.

2 Select important material to be remembered and using several of the methods outlined on pages 188–191 commence your revision. The method which produced the highest level of recall is the one that suits your study style.

3 Produce a set of crib cards (review page 192) for one subject area. Review your crib cards against the original sources. How accurately do they reflect the key issues?

4 It is difficult to identify what degree of stress or nervousness is problematic. However, using the comments on pages 197–199 try to:

a) clarify why a particular situation might cause you anxiety or stress

b) adopt the strategies recommended on pages 197–199 or your own strategies to combat the problem(s).

5 Try to identify objectively any mistakes you make in examinations. List these and using the material provided in this chapter develop a detailed plan to overcome them.

References

Acres, D. (2000) *How To Pass Exams Without Anxiety* (5th edition), How To Books

Bell, J., (2003) Doing Your Research Project, *A guide for First-Time Researchers in Education And Social Science* (3rd edition), Open University Press

Bowden, J. (2004) *Writing a Report* (7th edition), How To Books

Buzan, T. (2003) *Use Your Head*, BBC Books

Buzan, T. and Buzan, B. (2003) *The Mind Map Book*, BBC Books

Cottrell, S. (2003) *The Study Skills Handbook* (2nd edition), Palgrave

De Bono, E. (1990) *Lateral Thinking*, BBC Books

De Bono, E. (2004) *Edward De Bono's Thinking Course*, BBC Books

Evans, M. (2004) *How To Pass Exams Every Time* (2nd edition), How To Books

Fairnbairn, G. and Winch, C. (1991) *Reading, Writing and Reasoning, A Guide for Students*, Open University Press

Hobson, B. and Scally, M. (1984) *Life Skills Teaching Programme No. 1*, Leeds University Press

King, G. (2004) *The Good Grammar Guide*, Harper Collins

Maddox, H. (1988) *How to Study*, Pan Books

Northledge, A. (2003) *The Good Study Guide*, Open University Press

Rawlinson, J.G. (1988) *Creative Thinking and Brainstorming*, Gower Business Skills

Redman, P. (2003) *Good Essay Writing, A Social Sciences Guide* (2nd edition), Open University Press

Rose, J. (2001) *The Mature Student's Guide to Writing*, Palgrave

Soles, D. (2005) *The Academic Essay - How to plan, draft, write and revise*, Studymates

Sweetman, D. (2003) *Writing Your Dissertation* (3rd edition), How To Books

Some more suggestions

Allen, R. (2002) *Punctuation*, Oxford University Press (One Step Ahead series)

Allen, R. (2002) *Spelling*, Oxford University Press (One Step Ahead series)

Bigwood, S. and Spore, M. (2003) *Presenting Numbers, Tables and Charts,* Oxford University Press (One Step Ahead series)

Billingham, J (2002) *Editing and Revising Text*, Oxford University Press (One Step Ahead series)

Bryson, B. (2004) *Bryson's Dictionary of Troublesome Words*, Penguin Books *The Economist Style Guide* (8th edition, 2003), *The Economist* in association with Profile Books

Greenbaum, S. (2000) *The Oxford Reference Grammar*, Oxford University Press

Cochrane, J. (2003) *Between You and I: A Little Book of Bad English*, Icon Books

Trask, R.L. (2004) *The Penguin Guide to Punctuation*, Penguin Books

Truss, L. (2003) *Eats, Shoots and Leaves*, Profile Books

Index